COMPLETE MICROSOFT WORD GUIDE FOR BEGINNERS

A step by step tutorials

Kane Schiller

Copyright

Table of Contents

Introduction

Michael had always been curious about technology but never quite mastered any of it. His friends often teased him about being "technologically challenged," especially when it came to using software like Microsoft Word. So, when he saw a book titled *"Complete Microsoft Word Guide for Beginners"* in a bookstore, he felt a mix of hope and skepticism.

Without hesitation, he bought the book, determined to finally conquer the software that had always intimidated him. But something strange happened the moment he got home and placed the book on his desk. The title seemed to shimmer under the light, and as Michael stared at it, he felt a surge of energy flow through him.

He sat down at his computer, the book still unopened beside him. On a whim, he opened Microsoft Word, half expecting to fumble through the menus as usual. But to his surprise, everything felt different. The moment his fingers touched the keyboard, it was as if the knowledge from the book had already seeped into his mind.

He knew exactly how to adjust the margins, format text, and insert images. He navigated through menus with ease, discovering advanced features like mail merge and macro creation. It was as if he had been using the program for years.

Michael's confidence grew with each click. He created professional-looking documents in minutes, added charts and graphs with precision, and even used shortcuts he didn't know existed. His friends, who had always mocked his struggles with Word, were stunned when he started helping them with their own documents.

"Where did you learn all this?" they asked, their voices filled with disbelief.

Michael glanced at the book still sitting on his desk, untouched yet somehow magical. He smiled and said, "Just a little light reading."

The book's secrets had become his own, and from that day on, Michael was no longer just the guy who struggled with technology. He was the one who mastered it, all thanks to a book he never even had to open.

Chapter 1: Introduction to Microsoft Word

What is Microsoft Word?

Microsoft Word is a powerful word processing software developed by Microsoft. It is widely used for creating, editing, formatting, and sharing documents. Whether you need to draft a simple letter, create a detailed report, or design a professional resume, Microsoft Word offers a range of tools and features to make the process efficient and user-friendly. Word is part of the Microsoft Office suite, which includes other popular programs like Excel and PowerPoint.

Navigating the Word Interface

When you first open Microsoft Word, you are presented with a user interface that includes various components designed to help you work efficiently.

Here are the main elements of the Word interface:

- **Title Bar:** Located at the top of the window, the title bar displays the name of your document and the program you are using.
- **Ribbon:** The ribbon is a toolbar that spans the top of the window and contains tabs such as Home, Insert, Design, Layout, References, Mailings, Review, and View. Each tab has a set of related commands.
- **Quick Access Toolbar:** This toolbar is located above the ribbon and provides quick access to commonly used commands, such as Save, Undo, and Redo. You can customize this toolbar to include the commands you use most often.
- **Document Area:** The large area below the ribbon is where you type and edit your document.
- **Status Bar:** Located at the bottom of the window, the status bar displays information about your document, such as the page number, word count, and language. You can customize the status bar to show different information.

- **Scroll Bars:** These are found on the right side and bottom of the window, allowing you to scroll vertically and horizontally through your document.

- **View Buttons:** Located at the bottom-right of the window, these buttons let you switch between different views of your document, such as Print Layout, Read Mode, and Web Layout.

Creating a New Document

Creating a new document in Microsoft Word is straightforward. Here are the steps to get started:

1. Open Microsoft Word: If Word is not already open, start the program from your desktop or Start menu.

2. Select a Blank Document: On the Word start screen, you will see options for creating a new document. Click on "Blank document" to start with a clean slate.

3. Use a Template: If you prefer to use a template, you can select one from the start screen. Templates provide pre-designed layouts for various types of documents, such as resumes, reports, and flyers.

Opening and Saving Documents

Opening and saving documents are fundamental tasks you will perform frequently in Microsoft Word. Here's how to do both:

Opening a Document

1. File Tab: Click on the File tab in the ribbon.

2. Open: Select "Open" from the menu.

3. Browse: Click on "Browse" to navigate to the location where your document is saved.

4. Select File: Choose the document you want to open and click "Open."

Saving a Document

1. Save: To save a new document, click on the File tab and select "Save As."

2. Choose Location: Choose where you want to save your document (e.g., OneDrive, This PC).

3. Enter Filename: Type a name for your document.

4. Save: Click "Save" to save your document.

For subsequent saves, you can simply click the Save icon in the Quick Access Toolbar or press `Ctrl + S` on your keyboard. This will update the existing file with your latest changes.

By mastering these basic tasks, you will be well on your way to becoming proficient in using Microsoft Word for a variety of documents.

What is Microsoft Word?

Microsoft Word is a powerful word processing software developed by Microsoft. It is part of the Microsoft Office suite, which includes other popular programs such as Excel, PowerPoint, and Outlook. Word is widely used for creating, editing, formatting, and sharing text documents. It offers a range of tools and features that make it suitable for a variety of purposes, from drafting simple letters to designing complex reports and professional resumes.

Key Features of Microsoft Word

- **User-Friendly Interface:** Word's interface is designed to be intuitive and easy to navigate, making it accessible for users of all skill levels.
- **Text Formatting:** You can easily format text using a wide array of fonts, sizes, colors, and styles. This includes bold, italics, underline, and more.
- **Paragraph Formatting:** Control the alignment, indentation, and spacing of paragraphs to enhance the readability and layout of your documents.
- **Styles and Templates:** Word comes with pre-designed styles and templates that allow you to quickly apply consistent formatting to your documents.
- **Graphics and Media:** Insert and format images, shapes, SmartArt, and other graphics to make your documents more visually appealing.
- **Tables and Charts:** Create and format tables and charts to organize and present data effectively.
- **Collaboration Tools:** Word includes features for tracking changes, adding comments, and co-

authoring documents in real-time, making it easy to collaborate with others.

- **Proofing Tools:** Built-in spelling and grammar checkers help you ensure that your documents are error-free.

- **Accessibility:** Word offers various tools and settings to make documents accessible to users with disabilities.

Uses of Microsoft Word

- **Business:** Create professional documents such as reports, proposals, memos, and business letters.
- **Education:** Draft essays, research papers, and study notes. Teachers can prepare lesson plans and handouts.
- **Personal:** Write personal letters, resumes, and creative writing pieces. Design invitations and newsletters.
- **Legal:** Prepare contracts, agreements, and legal briefs with formatting that meets industry standards.

Microsoft Word is a versatile tool that has become the standard for word processing across various industries and sectors. Its comprehensive set of features and ease of use make it an essential software for anyone who needs to create, edit, and manage text documents.

Navigating the Word Interface

When you first open Microsoft Word, you are presented with a user-friendly interface designed to help you create and edit documents efficiently. Understanding the main components of this interface is crucial for getting the most out of Word.

Here are the key elements:

Title Bar
- **Location:** At the very top of the window.
- **Function:** Displays the name of your document and the program you are using. It also includes the control buttons (Minimize, Maximize/Restore, and Close) for the window.

Ribbon
- **Location:** Below the title bar.

- **Function:** A toolbar that organizes Word's features into a set of tabs. Each tab (Home, Insert, Design, Layout, References, Mailings, Review, View) contains related commands and tools.

- **Tabs:**

- **Home:** Includes basic text formatting tools like font, size, color, alignment, and styles.

- **Insert:** Allows you to add elements like tables, pictures, shapes, links, headers, footers, and page numbers.

- **Design:** Provides themes, colors, and font sets to customize the look of your document.

- **Layout:** Controls page setup, including margins, orientation, size, columns, and breaks.

- **References:** Manages citations, bibliographies, footnotes, endnotes, and table of contents.

- **Mailings:** Tools for mail merge operations like envelopes, labels, and merge fields.

- **Review:** Contains proofing tools, comments, track changes, and language settings.

- **View:** Allows you to change the document view, such as read mode, print layout, web layout, and zoom options.

Quick Access Toolbar

- **Location:** Above the ribbon, usually in the top-left corner.
- **Function:** Provides quick access to frequently used commands like Save, Undo, Redo, and Print. You can customize it to include other commands you use often.

Document Area

- **Location:** The large central area below the ribbon.
- **Function:** This is where you type and edit your document. It displays the text and elements as they will appear in the final document.

Status Bar

- **Location:** At the bottom of the window.
- **Function:** Displays information about your document, such as page number, word count, and language. It also includes view buttons and a zoom slider for changing the document's view and zoom level.

Scroll Bars

- **Location:** On the right side and bottom of the document area.

- **Function:** Allow you to scroll vertically and horizontally through your document. You can click and drag the scroll boxes or use the arrows at either end.

View Buttons

- **Location:** In the bottom-right corner of the window, within the status bar.

- **Function:** These buttons let you switch between different views of your document:

  - **Read Mode:** Optimizes the document for reading, hiding the ribbon and other tools.

  - **Print Layout:** Shows how the document will look when printed, with all formatting and page layout.

  - **Web Layout:** Displays the document as it would appear in a web browser.

Zoom Slider

- **Location:** In the status bar, next to the view buttons.

- **Function:** Allows you to zoom in and out of your document for a closer or wider view.

Backstage View (File Tab)

- Location: The first tab on the ribbon.

- Function: Provides access to document management tasks like saving, opening, closing, printing, and sharing documents. It also includes options for document properties and Word settings.

By familiarizing yourself with these components, you can navigate Microsoft Word more effectively and utilize its features to create and edit your documents with ease.

Creating a New Document

Creating a new document in Microsoft Word is a straightforward process that allows you to start with a clean slate or use a pre-designed template.

how to create a new document in both ways:

Creating a New Blank Document

1. Open Microsoft Word:

- If Word is not already open, start the program from your desktop shortcut, Start menu, or taskbar.

2. New Document Options:

- Upon opening Word, you will be presented with the start screen. This screen offers options to open recent documents or create a new document.

3. Select Blank Document:

- Click on the "Blank document" option, typically located at the top of the start screen. This will open a new, untitled document where you can begin typing and formatting your content.

4. Begin Working:

- Once the new blank document opens, you can start typing and using Word's various tools and features to format and enhance your text.

Creating a New Document from a Template

Microsoft Word offers a variety of templates that provide pre-designed layouts for different types of documents, such as resumes, reports, flyers, and more. Using a template can save you time and ensure a professional look.

how to create a new document using a template:

1. Open Microsoft Word:
  - Start the program if it's not already open.

2. Access Templates:
  - On the start screen, in addition to the "Blank document" option, you will see a variety of templates. If you don't see the template you need, click on "More templates" to browse the full library.

3. Browse Templates:
  - Use the search bar at the top of the templates section to search for a specific type of template (e.g., "resume," "invoice," "newsletter"). You can also browse by category.

4. Select a Template:
  - Click on a template to preview it. If you find one that suits your needs, click the "Create" button. This

will open a new document based on the selected template.

5. Customize the Template:
- Once the new document opens, you can customize it by replacing the placeholder text and images with your own content. You can also modify the formatting to better fit your needs.

Saving Your New Document

After creating a new document, whether from scratch or from a template, it's important to save your work regularly to prevent data loss.

Here's how to save your document:

1. Save As:
- For a new document that hasn't been saved before, click on the File tab in the ribbon and select "Save As."

2. Choose Location:

- Choose where you want to save your document. You can save it to your computer, OneDrive, or another location. Click on "Browse" to navigate to the desired folder.

3. Enter Filename:

- Type a name for your document in the "File name" field.

4. Select File Format:

- Choose the file format for your document (e.g., Word Document (*.docx), PDF (.pdf)). The default format is typically fine for most purposes.

5. Save:

- Click the "Save" button to save your document.

For subsequent saves, you can simply click the Save icon in the Quick Access Toolbar or press `Ctrl + S` on your keyboard. This will update the existing file with your latest changes.

By following these steps, you can easily create new documents in Microsoft Word, whether you're starting from scratch or using a template. Regularly saving your work ensures that you won't lose any important changes.

Opening and Saving Documents

Opening and saving documents are fundamental tasks you will perform frequently in Microsoft Word.

Here's how to do both:

Opening a Document

To open an existing document in Microsoft Word, follow these steps:

1. File Tab:
   - Click on the **File** tab in the ribbon, located at the top-left corner of the window.

2. Open:

- Select **Open** from the menu. This will bring up the Open screen, where you can choose from a list of recent documents or browse for a file.

3. Browse:

- Click on **Browse** to navigate to the location where your document is saved. This will open the File Explorer (Windows) or Finder (Mac).

4. Select File:

- Locate the document you want to open, click on it to select it, and then click the **Open** button. Alternatively, you can double-click the file to open it.

5. Recent Documents:

- If you have recently worked on the document, you can select it directly from the list of recent documents on the Open screen.

Saving a Document

Saving your document regularly is crucial to prevent data loss.

How to save your work in Microsoft Word:

Saving a New Document

1. Save As:

  - If you are saving a new document for the first time, click on the **File** tab and select **Save As.**

2. Choose Location:

  - Choose where you want to save your document. You can save it to your computer, OneDrive, or another cloud storage service. Click on **Browse** to navigate to the desired folder.

3. Enter Filename:

  - Type a name for your document in the **File name** field.

4. Select File Format:

  - Choose the file format for your document (e.g., Word Document **(.docx)**, PDF **(.pdf))**. The default format is typically fine for most purposes.

5. Save:

- Click the **Save** button to save your document.

Saving an Existing Document

1. Save:

- For subsequent saves, simply click the **Save** icon in the Quick Access Toolbar or press `Ctrl + S` (Windows) or `Command + S` (Mac) on your keyboard. This will update the existing file with your latest changes.

Save As for a Copy

1. Save As:

- If you want to save a copy of the document with a different name or location, click on the **File** tab and select **Save As.**

2. Enter New Filename:

- Enter a new name for the document to create a copy.

3. Choose Location:

- Select the location where you want to save the copy.

4. Save:

 - Click the **Save** button to save the new copy of the document.

AutoSave Feature

Microsoft Word also includes an AutoSave feature that automatically saves your document at regular intervals. This is especially useful when working on long or complex documents.

1. Enable AutoSave:

 - To enable AutoSave, ensure your document is saved to OneDrive or SharePoint. The AutoSave toggle switch is located in the top-left corner of the window, near the title bar.

By mastering these basic tasks, you can ensure that your documents are safely stored and easily accessible whenever you need them. Regularly saving your work and using the AutoSave feature can help prevent data loss and give you peace of mind.

Chapter 2: Basic Document Formatting

Text Formatting Basics

Text formatting is essential for making your document clear and professional. Microsoft Word offers various tools to format text, such as changing fonts, adjusting sizes, and applying styles like bold or italics.

Changing Fonts and Sizes

1. Selecting Text:
   - Highlight the text you want to format. You can do this by clicking and dragging your mouse over the text or by double-clicking on a word to select it.

2. Font:
   - In the **Home** tab, locate the **Font** group.
   - Click the **Font** drop-down menu to select a different font. Popular choices include Arial, Times New Roman, and Calibri.

3. Font Size:

- Next to the Font drop-down menu, there is a **Font Size** menu. Click the drop-down arrow to select a different size or type a specific size into the box.

Applying Bold, Italics, and Underline

1. Bold:

- Select the text you want to bold. In the **Home** tab, click the **Bold** button (B) in the **Font** group or press `Ctrl + B` (Windows) or `Command + B` (Mac) on your keyboard.

2. Italics:

- Select the text you want to italicize. Click the **Italics** button (I) in the **Font** group or press `Ctrl + I` (Windows) or `Command + I` (Mac).

3. Underline:

- Select the text you want to underline. Click the **Underline** button (U) in the **Font** group or press `Ctrl + U` (Windows) or `Command + U` (Mac).

Changing Text Color

1. Text Color:
- Select the text you want to change. In the **Home** tab, click the **Font Color** button, which looks like an "A" with a colored underline.
- Choose a color from the palette or click **More Colors** for additional options.

Highlighting Text

1. Text Highlight Color:
- Select the text you want to highlight. In the **Home** tab, click the **Text Highlight Color** button, which looks like a marker pen.
- Choose a highlight color from the palette.

Paragraph Formatting

Paragraph formatting involves adjusting the alignment, indentation, and spacing of paragraphs to enhance the readability and layout of your document.

Aligning Text

1. Left Align:

- Select the paragraph you want to align. In the **Home** tab, click the **Align Left** button or press `Ctrl + L` (Windows) or `Command + L` (Mac).

2. Center Align:

- Select the paragraph you want to center. Click the **Center** button or press `Ctrl + E` (Windows) or `Command + E` (Mac).

3. Right Align:

- Select the paragraph you want to align to the right. Click the **Align Right** button or press `Ctrl + R` (Windows) or `Command + R` (Mac).

4. Justify:

- Select the paragraph you want to justify. Click the **Justify** button or press `Ctrl + J` (Windows) or `Command + J` (Mac). Justified text is aligned evenly along both the left and right margins.

Indenting Paragraphs

1. Increase Indent:

- Select the paragraph you want to indent. In the **Home** tab, click the **Increase Indent** button, which looks like an arrow pointing to the right.

2. Decrease Indent:

- To reduce the indentation, click the **Decrease Indent** button, which looks like an arrow pointing to the left.

Adjusting Line Spacing

1. Line and Paragraph Spacing:

- Select the paragraph you want to adjust. In the **Home** tab, click the **Line and Paragraph Spacing** button, which looks like lines with up and down arrows.
- Choose a spacing option from the drop-down menu. Common choices include 1.0 (single spacing), 1.5, and 2.0 (double spacing).

2. Custom Spacing:

- For more precise control, select **Line Spacing Options** from the drop-down menu. This opens a dialog box where you can set specific values for line spacing and add space before or after paragraphs.

Adding Bullets and Numbering

1. Bulleted Lists:
   - Select the text you want to turn into a bulleted list. In the **Home** tab, click the **Bullets** button in the **Paragraph** group.

2. Numbered Lists:
   - Select the text you want to turn into a numbered list. Click the **Numbering** button in the **Paragraph** group.

3. Customizing Lists:
   - Click the drop-down arrow next to the Bullets or Numbering button to choose different bullet styles or number formats. Select **Define New Bullet** or **Define New Number Format** for more customization options.

Working with Styles

Styles are pre-defined combinations of formatting that you can apply to text to ensure consistent and professional-looking documents.

Applying Styles

1. Styles Gallery:
   - In the **Home** tab, locate the **Styles** group. This includes a gallery of styles like Normal, Heading 1, Heading 2, and more.

2. Apply a Style:
   - Select the text you want to format. Click on a style in the gallery to apply it. For example, applying the "Heading 1" style will format your text as a main heading.

Modifying Styles

1. Modify a Style:

- Right-click on a style in the Styles gallery and select **Modify.** This opens the Modify Style dialog box.

2. Adjust Formatting:

- In the Modify Style dialog box, you can change the font, size, color, alignment, and other formatting options. Click **OK** to save your changes.

Creating New Styles

1. Create a New Style:

- In the **Styles** group, click the **More** button (a small arrow in the bottom-right corner) to open the Styles pane.
- Click the **New Style** button at the bottom of the Styles pane.

2. Define Style:

- In the Create New Style from Formatting dialog box, name your new style and define its formatting options. Click **OK** to save your new style.

Page Layout and Margins

Proper page layout and margins are essential for creating well-structured documents.

Setting Page Margins

1. Margins:

- In the **Layout** tab, click the **Margins** button in the **Page Setup** group.

- Choose from preset margin options (Normal, Narrow, Moderate, Wide) or click **Custom Margins** to set specific values.

Changing Page Orientation

1. Orientation:

- In the **Layout** tab, click the **Orientation** button in the **Page Setup** group.

- Select either **Portrait** (vertical) or **Landscape** (horizontal) orientation.

Adjusting Page Size

1. Size:

- In the **Layout** tab, click the **Size** button in the **Page Setup** group.

- Choose from preset page sizes (Letter, A4, Legal) or click **More Paper Sizes** to enter custom dimensions.

Adding Headers and Footers

1. Headers and Footers:

- In the **Insert** tab, click the **Header** or **Footer** button in the **Header & Footer** group.

- Choose from preset header and footer designs or click **Edit Header** or **Edit Footer** to customize.

2. Inserting Page Numbers:

- Click the **Page Number** button in the **Insert** tab and choose a location for your page numbers (Top of Page, Bottom of Page, Page Margins).

- Customize the format and position as needed.

By mastering these basic formatting techniques, you can create well-organized, visually appealing documents in Microsoft Word. Proper text and paragraph formatting, the use of styles, and thoughtful page layout settings will make your documents professional and easy to read.

Text Formatting Basics

Text formatting is essential for making your document clear and professional. Microsoft Word offers various tools to format text, such as changing fonts, adjusting sizes, and applying styles like bold or italics. Here's a detailed guide on how to use these features.

Changing Fonts and Sizes

1. Selecting Text:
   - Highlight the text you want to format by clicking and dragging your mouse over it or by double-clicking on a word to select it.

2. Font:
   - In the **Home** tab, locate the **Font** group.
   - Click the **Font** drop-down menu to select a different font. Popular choices include Arial, Times New Roman, and Calibri.

3. Font Size:

- Next to the Font drop-down menu, there is a **Font Size** menu. Click the drop-down arrow to select a different size or type a specific size into the box.

Applying Bold, Italics, and Underline

1. Bold:

- Select the text you want to bold. In the **Home** tab, click the **Bold** button (B) in the **Font** group or press `Ctrl + B` (Windows) or `Command + B` (Mac) on your keyboard.

2. Italics:

- Select the text you want to italicize. Click the **Italics** button (I) in the **Font** group or press `Ctrl + I` (Windows) or `Command + I` (Mac).

3. Underline:

- Select the text you want to underline. Click the **Underline** button (U) in the **Font** group or press `Ctrl + U` (Windows) or `Command + U` (Mac).

Changing Text Color

1. Text Color:

- Select the text you want to change. In the **Home** tab, click the **Font Color** button, which looks like an "A" with a colored underline.

- Choose a color from the palette or click **More Colors** for additional options.

Highlighting Text

1. Text Highlight Color:

- Select the text you want to highlight. In the **Home** tab, click the **Text Highlight Color** button, which looks like a marker pen.

- Choose a highlight color from the palette.

Strikethrough and Subscript/Superscript

1. Strikethrough:

- Select the text you want to strike through. In the **Home** tab, click the **Strikethrough** button (abc with a line through it).

2. Subscript:

   - Select the text you want to format as subscript. In the **Home** tab, click the **Subscript** button (x_2) or press `Ctrl + =` (Windows) or `Command + =` (Mac).

3. Superscript:

   - Select the text you want to format as superscript. In the **Home** tab, click the **Superscript** button (x^2) or press `Ctrl + Shift + =` (Windows) or `Command + Shift + =` (Mac).

Using the Font Dialog Box

For more advanced text formatting options, you can use the Font dialog box. Here's how to access and use it:

1. Open Font Dialog Box:

   - In the **Home** tab, click the small arrow in the bottom-right corner of the **Font** group. This opens the Font dialog box.

2. Font Tab:

- In the Font tab, you can change the font, style (regular, bold, italic), size, color, underline style, and effects (strikethrough, double strikethrough, superscript, subscript, shadow, outline, emboss, engrave, small caps, all caps, hidden).

3. Advanced Tab:

- The Advanced tab allows you to adjust character spacing (scale, spacing, position) and OpenType features (ligatures, number spacing, number forms).

4. Preview:

- The Preview section at the bottom of the dialog box shows how your text will look with the selected formatting options.

5. Apply Changes:

- After making your selections, click **OK** to apply the changes to your text.

Clearing Formatting

If you need to remove all formatting from a section of text, you can use the Clear Formatting option:

1. Select Text:

- Highlight the text you want to clear formatting from.

2. Clear Formatting:

- In the **Home** tab, click the **Clear Formatting** button (an eraser icon) in the **Font** group. This will reset the text to the default font and size.

By mastering these text formatting basics, you can create documents that are visually appealing and easy to read. Consistent and appropriate use of fonts, sizes, colors, and styles will enhance the overall professionalism of your documents.

Paragraph Formatting

Paragraph formatting involves adjusting the alignment, indentation, and spacing of paragraphs to enhance the readability and layout of your document. Microsoft Word provides several tools to help you format paragraphs effectively.

Aligning Text

1. Left Align:
  - Select the paragraph you want to align. In the **Home** tab, click the **Align Left** button in the **Paragraph** group or press `Ctrl + L` (Windows) or `Command + L` (Mac).

2. Center Align:
  - Select the paragraph you want to center. Click the **Center** button in the **Paragraph** group or press `Ctrl + E` (Windows) or `Command + E` (Mac).

3. Right Align:
  - Select the paragraph you want to align to the right. Click the **Align Right** button in the **Paragraph** group or press `Ctrl + R` (Windows) or `Command + R` (Mac).

4. Justify:

- Select the paragraph you want to justify. Click the **Justify** button in the **Paragraph** group or press `Ctrl + J` (Windows) or `Command + J` (Mac). Justified text is aligned evenly along both the left and right margins.

Indenting Paragraphs

1. Increase Indent:

- Select the paragraph you want to indent. In the **Home** tab, click the **Increase Indent** button, which looks like an arrow pointing to the right.

2. Decrease Indent:

- To reduce the indentation, click the **Decrease Indent** button, which looks like an arrow pointing to the left.

3. First Line Indent:

- To indent only the first line of a paragraph, place your cursor at the beginning of the line. In the **Home** tab, open the **Paragraph** dialog box by clicking the small arrow in the bottom-right corner of the **Paragraph** group. Under **Indentation**, select

First line from the **Special** drop-down menu and set the desired indent value.

4. Hanging Indent:

- For a hanging indent, where the first line is not indented but all subsequent lines are, open the **Paragraph** dialog box, select **Hanging** from the **Special** drop-down menu, and set the desired indent value.

Adjusting Line Spacing

1. Line and Paragraph Spacing:

- Select the paragraph you want to adjust. In the **Home** tab, click the **Line and Paragraph Spacing** button, which looks like lines with up and down arrows.

- Choose a spacing option from the drop-down menu. Common choices include 1.0 (single spacing), 1.5, and 2.0 (double spacing).

2. Custom Spacing:

- For more precise control, select **Line Spacing Options** from the drop-down menu. This opens a dialog box where you can set specific values for line spacing and add space before or after paragraphs.

Adding Bullets and Numbering

1. Bulleted Lists:

   - Select the text you want to turn into a bulleted list. In the **Home tab,** click the **Bullets** button in the **Paragraph** group.

2. Numbered Lists:

   - Select the text you want to turn into a numbered list. Click the **Numbering** button in the **Paragraph** group.

3. Customizing Lists:

   - Click the drop-down arrow next to the Bullets or Numbering button to choose different bullet styles or number formats. Select **Define New Bullet** or **Define New Number Format** for more customization options.

4. Multilevel Lists:

- For more complex lists, click the **Multilevel List** button in the **Paragraph** group. This allows you to create hierarchical lists with multiple levels of bullets or numbering.

Adding Borders and Shading

1. Borders:
   - Select the paragraph you want to add a border to. In the **Hom** tab, click the **Borders** button in the **Paragraph** group. Choose from options like **Bottom Border**, **Top Border**, **All Borders**, and more.

2. Shading:
   - To add shading to a paragraph, select the paragraph and click the **Shading** button in the **Paragraph** group. Choose a shading color from the palette.

Controlling Widows and Orphans

Widows and orphans refer to single lines of text at the beginning or end of a paragraph that are left stranded at the top or bottom of a page. To prevent this, use the following steps:

1. Paragraph Dialog Box:
   - Open the **Paragraph** dialog box by clicking the small arrow in the bottom-right corner of the **Paragraph** group in the **Home** tab.

2. Line and Page Breaks:
   - In the **Paragraph** dialog box, go to the **Line and Page Breaks** tab.

3. Widow/Orphan Control:
   - Check the **Widow/Orphan control** box to prevent single lines of text from being stranded at the top or bottom of a page.

Adjusting Paragraph Spacing

1. Before and After Spacing:
   - To add or remove space before or after a paragraph, open the **Paragraph** dialog box. Under **Spacing**, adjust the values in the **Before** and **After** fields.

2. Default Spacing:

- To set default spacing for all new documents, click the **Set As Default** button in the **Paragraph** dialog box and choose **All documents based on the Normal template.**

By mastering these paragraph formatting techniques, you can create well-organized, visually appealing documents in Microsoft Word. Proper text and paragraph formatting, the use of styles, and thoughtful page layout settings will make your documents professional and easy to read.

Working with Styles

Styles are pre-defined combinations of formatting that you can apply to text to ensure consistent and professional-looking documents. Microsoft Word provides various built-in styles and allows you to create and modify your own styles.

Applying Styles

1. Styles Gallery:

- In the **Home** tab, locate the **Styles** group. This includes a gallery of styles like Normal, Heading 1, Heading 2, and more.

2. Apply a Style:

- Select the text you want to format. Click on a style in the gallery to apply it. For example, applying the "Heading 1" style will format your text as a main heading.

Modifying Styles

1. Modify a Style:

- Right-click on a style in the Styles gallery and select **Modify**. This opens the Modify Style dialog box.

2. Adjust Formatting:

- In the Modify Style dialog box, you can change the font, size, color, alignment, and other formatting options. Click **OK** to save your changes.

Creating New Styles

1. Create a New Style:

- In the **Styles** group, click the **More** button (a small arrow in the bottom-right corner) to open the Styles pane.

- Click the **New Style** button at the bottom of the Styles pane.

2. Define Style:

- In the Create New Style from Formatting dialog box, name your new style and define its formatting options. Click **OK** to save your new style.

Using the Styles Pane

The Styles pane provides a more comprehensive view of the styles available in your document and allows for easier management of styles.

1. Open Styles Pane:

- In the **Home** tab, click the small arrow in the bottom-right corner of the **Styles** group to open the Styles pane.

2. Apply Styles from the Pane:

- To apply a style, select the text you want to format and click on the desired style in the Styles pane.

3. Manage Styles:

- The Styles pane also allows you to manage styles by right-clicking on a style and selecting options like **Modify**, **Delete**, or **Update to Match Selection.**

Creating a Table of Contents with Styles

Using styles, especially for headings, allows you to create a Table of Contents (TOC) easily.

1. Apply Heading Styles:

- Ensure that you have applied heading styles (Heading 1, Heading 2, etc.) to the headings in your document.

2. Insert TOC:

- Place your cursor where you want to insert the TOC. Go to the **References** tab and click the **Table**

of Contents button in the **Table of Contents** group.

3. Choose TOC Style:

- Select a TOC style from the gallery. Word will generate the TOC based on the heading styles in your document.

4. Update TOC:

- If you make changes to your document, you can update the TOC by clicking it and selecting **Update Table.** Choose to update page numbers only or the entire table.

Using Style Sets

Style Sets are collections of styles that are designed to work together to create a cohesive look for your document.

1. Apply a Style Set:

- In the **Design** tab, locate the **Document Formatting** group.

- Click on a Style Set to apply it to your document. This will change the appearance of all the styles in your document to match the selected set.

2. Customize a Style Set:
- After applying a Style Set, you can still modify individual styles to further customize your document's appearance.

Saving Custom Style Sets

If you frequently use a specific set of styles, you can save it as a custom Style Set.

1. Customize Styles:
- Modify the styles in your document as desired.

2. Save as a Style Set:
- In the **Design** tab, click the **More** button in the **Document Formatting** group.
- Select **Save as a New Style Set.**

- Name your Style Set and click **Save**. Your custom Style Set will now be available in the gallery for future use.

Clearing Styles

If you need to remove all styles from a section of text, you can clear formatting:

1. Select Text:
- Highlight the text you want to clear the style from.

2. Clear Formatting:
- In the **Home** tab, click the **Clear Formatting** button (an eraser icon) in the **Font** group. This will reset the text to the default font and size.

By mastering the use of styles in Microsoft Word, you can create documents that are not only visually appealing but also consistently formatted. Styles help maintain uniformity across large documents and make it easier to manage and update formatting.

Page Layout and Margins

Proper page layout and margins are essential for creating well-structured and visually appealing documents in Microsoft Word. Here's how you can adjust page layout settings to suit your needs.

Setting Page Margins

1. Margins:

- In the **Layout** tab, click the **Margins** button in the **Page Setup** group.

- Choose from preset margin options such as Normal, Narrow, Moderate, or Wide. Alternatively, click **Custom Margins** to set specific margin values.

2. Custom Margins:

- If you choose **Custom Margins**, the Page Setup dialog box will appear.

- Here, you can set precise measurements for Top, Bottom, Left, and Right margins. You can also adjust the Gutter and Orientation (Portrait or Landscape).

Changing Page Orientation

1. Orientation:

- In the **Layout** tab, click the **Orientation** button in the **Page Setup** group.

- Select **Portrait** (vertical) or **Landscape** (horizontal) orientation as per your document's requirements.

Adjusting Page Size

1. Size:

- In the **Layout** tab, click the **Size** button in the **Page Setup** group.

- Choose from standard page sizes like Letter, Legal, A4, etc. You can also select **More Paper Sizes** to enter custom dimensions.

Adding Headers and Footers

1. Headers and Footers:

- In the **Insert** tab, click either **Header** or **Footer** in the **Header & Footer** group.

- Choose a built-in header or footer style, or click **Edit Header** or **Edit Footer** to create a custom header or footer for your document.

2. Inserting Page Numbers:

- While in the header or footer area, click the **Page Number** button in the **Header & Footer** group.

- Choose the position and format of the page numbers. You can select **Top of Page, Bottom of Page,** or **Page Margins** for placement.

Controlling Page Breaks

1. Page Breaks:

- To insert a manual page break, place the cursor where you want the new page to begin.

- In the **Insert** tab, click the **Page Break** button in the **Pages** group. This will move all content after the cursor to the next page.

2. Section Breaks:

- For more complex page layout changes, such as changing margins or orientation within the same document, use **Section Breaks.**

- In the **Layout** tab, click the **Breaks** button in the **Page Setup** group. Choose from **Next Page, Continuous, Even Page,** or **Odd Page** breaks.

Adding Columns

1. Columns:

- In the **Layout** tab, click the **Columns** button in the **Page Setup** group.

- Choose the number of columns you want to divide your text into, or select **More Columns** for additional options such as column width and spacing.

Applying Watermarks

1. Watermarks:

- In the **Design** tab (or **Page Layout** tab in older versions), click the **Watermark** button in the **Page Background** group.

- Choose from built-in watermarks like **Confidential, Urgent**, or **Draft**, or click **Custom Watermark** to create your own watermark.

Printing Options

1. Print Preview:
- Before printing, you can preview your document by clicking **File** > **Print** and selecting **Print Preview.** This allows you to see how your document will look when printed.

2. Page Setup for Printing:
- In the **Print** dialog box, you can adjust settings such as page orientation, paper size, margins, and scaling under **Printer Properties** or **Settings** depending on your printer.

By mastering these page layout and margin settings in Microsoft Word, you can customize your document's appearance to meet specific requirements. Properly adjusted margins, orientations, headers, and footers enhance readability and ensure your document looks professional and polished.

Chapter 3: Working with Graphics and Tables

Graphics and tables are essential elements for enhancing the visual appeal and organizing information in Microsoft Word documents. Here's how you can effectively work with graphics and tables to create professional-looking documents.

Inserting and Formatting Graphics

1. Inserting Pictures:

- Place your cursor where you want to insert the picture.

- In the **Insert** tab, click the **Pictures** button in the **Illustrations** group.

- Navigate to the location of your image file, select it, and click **Insert**.

2. Inserting Shapes:

- Shapes can be useful for creating diagrams or highlighting specific information.

- In the **Insert** tab, click the **Shapes** button in the **Illustrations** group. Choose a shape from the gallery and draw it in your document.

3. Formatting Graphics:

- After inserting a graphic, you can format it using the **Format** tab that appears when the graphic is selected.
- Use options like **Wrap Text** to control how text flows around the graphic, adjust **Position** to place it precisely on the page, and apply **Styles** or **Effects** to enhance its appearance.

4. Adding Captions:

- To add a caption to a picture, select the picture, then click the **References** tab.
- Click **Insert Caption** in the **Captions** group, type your caption, and click **OK**.

Inserting and Formatting Tables

1. Inserting Tables:

- Place your cursor where you want to insert the table.

- In the **Insert** tab, click the **Table** button. You can draw a custom table or select **Insert Table** to specify the number of rows and columns.

2. Formatting Tables:

- After inserting a table, the **Table Tools** tabs (**Design** and **Layout**) appear.

- Use these tabs to apply styles, adjust borders and shading, and customize the layout of your table.

3. Adding and Removing Rows and Columns:

- To add or remove rows and columns, place your cursor in a cell within the table.

- In the **Layout** tab under **Rows & Columns,** use the **Insert Above, Insert Below, Insert Left, Insert Right, Delete Row, and Delete Column** options.

4. Merging and Splitting Cells:

- You can merge cells to create headers or combine data. Select the cells you want to merge, right-click, and choose **Merge Cells.**

- To split cells, select a cell or cells, right-click, and choose **Split Cells.**

Importing Data from Excel

1. Copying and Pasting:
  - If you have data in an Excel spreadsheet that you want to include in your Word document, select the cells in Excel, copy them (`Ctrl + C`), switch to Word, and paste (`Ctrl + V`) them into your document.

2. Linking Excel Data:
  - You can also link Excel data to Word, so changes in the Excel file are automatically updated in the Word document.
  - Copy the data in Excel, switch to Word, and use **Paste Special** (`Ctrl + Alt + V`) to choose **Paste Link**. Any changes made in Excel will reflect in Word when you update the link.

Adding Charts

1. Inserting Charts:
  - Charts are useful for visualizing data. Place your cursor where you want to insert the chart.

- In the **Insert** tab, click the **Chart** button in the **Illustrations** group. Choose the type of chart you want and click **OK**.

2. Formatting Charts**:

- After inserting a chart, the **Chart Tools** tabs (**Design, Layout,** and **Format**) appear.
- Use these tabs to change the chart type, apply chart styles, add or remove chart elements (like axes, titles, and legends), and format the chart's appearance.

Grouping and Aligning Objects

1. Grouping Objects:

- To group multiple objects (such as shapes or pictures) together so they can be moved and formatted as a single unit, select them all, right-click, and choose **Group > Group.**

2. Aligning Objects:

- To align objects (pictures, shapes, etc.) relative to each other or to the page margins, select the objects, then go to the **Format** tab.

- Use the **Align** and **Distribute** options in the **Arrange** group to align objects vertically or horizontally, distribute them evenly, or align them to the page.

Adding SmartArt Graphics

1. Inserting SmartArt:
 - SmartArt graphics are visual representations of information and ideas. Place your cursor where you want to insert the SmartArt graphic.
 - In the **Insert** tab, click the **SmartArt** button in the **Illustrations** group. Choose a SmartArt graphic category and select a layout that suits your needs.

2. Editing SmartArt:
 - After inserting a SmartArt graphic, use the **SmartArt Tools** tabs (**Design, Format,** and **Arrange**) to add text, change colors and styles, rearrange shapes, and customize the graphic.

By effectively utilizing graphics and tables in your Microsoft Word documents, you can enhance the presentation of information, improve readability, and create visually engaging materials for various purposes.

Inserting and Formatting Images

Adding images to your Microsoft Word documents can enhance visual appeal and effectively convey information.

The step-by-step guide on how to insert and format images in Word:

Inserting Images

1. Inserting Pictures from File:

 - Place your cursor where you want to insert the image.

 - Go to the **Insert** tab.

 - Click on the **Pictures** button in the **Illustrations** group.

 - Navigate to the location of your image file on your computer.

- Select the image file and click **Insert**.

2. Inserting Online Pictures:

- If you want to insert a picture from an online source (like Bing Image Search or OneDrive), go to the **Insert** tab and click **Online Pictures** in the **Illustrations** group.

- Use the search box to find the image you want, select it, and click **Insert**.

3. Inserting Screenshots:

- To insert a screenshot of your computer screen, go to the **Insert** tab and click **Screenshot** in the **Illustrations** group.

- Choose the window or screen you want to capture. Word will insert the screenshot directly into your document.

Resizing and Moving Images

1. Resizing Images:

- Click on the image to select it.
- Use the corner sizing handles (small squares) to drag and resize the image proportionally. Hold the

Shift key while resizing to maintain the image's aspect ratio.

2. Moving Images:

- Click and drag the image to move it to a different location within your document.

Wrapping Text around Images

1. Text Wrapping Options:

- After inserting an image, select it.
- Go to the **Format** tab (or the **Picture Format** tab in newer versions).
- In the **Arrange** group, click **Wrap Text** to see different wrapping options:

   - **In Line with Text:** The image stays in line with the text, and text wraps around it.

   - **Square:** Text wraps around the rectangular border of the image.

   - **Tight:** Text wraps closely around the shape of the image.

   - **Behind Text:** The image is placed behind the text.

- In Front of Text: The image is placed in front of the text.

2. Adjusting Text Wrapping:

- Choose the text wrapping style that suits your document layout by clicking on the desired option.

Formatting Images

1. Picture Styles:

- With the image selected, go to the **Format** (or **Picture Format**) tab.
- Use the **Picture Styles** gallery to apply predefined styles to your image, such as borders, shadows, reflections, and more.

2. Adjusting Picture Corrections and Color:

- In the **Format** (or **Picture Format****) tab, use the **Corrections** and **Color** options to adjust brightness, contrast, sharpness, and color saturation of the image.

3. Adding Borders and Effects:

- To add a border around the image, click **Picture Border** in the **Format** (or **Picture Format**) tab and choose a border style and color.

- Use **Picture Effects** to apply artistic effects like shadows, reflections, glow, and more.

Adding Alt Text

1. Alt Text for Accessibility:

- Right-click on the image and select **Edit Alt Text.**

- In the **Alt Text** pane, provide a brief, descriptive title and description for the image. This helps users with visual impairments understand the content of the image.

Grouping Images

1. Grouping Images:

- To group multiple images together so they can be moved and formatted as a single unit, select all the images by holding down the Ctrl key and clicking on each image.

- Right-click and choose **Group > Group.** Now you can move and format them together.

Saving and Compressing Images

1. Saving Images:
   - If you've inserted an image into your document and need to save it separately, right-click the image and select **Save as Picture.**

2. Compressing Images:
   - Large images can increase the size of your Word document. To reduce the file size, select the image, go to the **Format** (or **Picture Format**) tab, click **Compress Pictures** in the **Adjust** group.
   - Choose your preferred options for compression (e.g., resolution) and click **OK**.

following these steps, you can effectively insert, format, and manage images in Microsoft Word to create visually appealing and professional-looking documents.

Adding Shapes and SmartArt

Adding Shapes and SmartArt in Microsoft Word

Microsoft Word allows you to enhance your documents by incorporating shapes and SmartArt graphics, which can visually represent information and concepts.

How you can add and work with shapes and SmartArt:

Adding Shapes

1. Inserting Basic Shapes:

 - Place your cursor where you want to insert the shape.

 - Go to the **Insert** tab.

 - Click on the **Shapes** button in the **Illustrations** group.

 - Choose a shape from the gallery (e.g., rectangles, circles, arrows) and click to insert it into your document.

2. Drawing Custom Shapes:

- If you need a specific shape not available in the gallery, click **New Drawing Canvas** in the **Shapes** gallery.

- Use the **Shapes** tools (like **Rectangle, Ellipse, Line**, etc.) in the **Format** tab under **Insert Shapes** to draw custom shapes.

3. Formatting Shapes:

- After inserting a shape, you can format it to suit your document's design.

- Click on the shape to select it.

- Use the options in the **Format** (or **Shape Format**) tab to change fill color, outline color, add effects, adjust shape properties, and more.

Adding SmartArt Graphics

1. Inserting SmartArt:

- SmartArt graphics are visual representations of information and ideas.

- Place your cursor where you want to insert the SmartArt graphic.

- Go to the **Insert** tab.

- Click on the **SmartArt** button in the **Illustrations** group.

2. Choosing a SmartArt Layout:

- In the **Choose a SmartArt Graphic** dialog box, browse through categories like **List, Process, Cycle, Hierarchy, Relationship, Matrix, Pyramid, or Picture.**

- Select a layout that best fits the content you want to represent and click **OK**.

3. Editing SmartArt:

- After inserting SmartArt, a new tab called **SmartArt Tools** appears with **Design, Format,** and **Arrange** tabs.

- Use these tabs to enter text, change colors, styles, add or remove shapes, and rearrange elements within the SmartArt graphic.

4. Adding Text to SmartArt:

- Click on a shape in the SmartArt graphic to enter text directly. The text will automatically adjust to fit within the shape.

5. Changing SmartArt Styles:

- In the **SmartArt Tools Design** tab, use the **SmartArt Styles** group to choose a different style for your SmartArt graphic. This can quickly change colors, effects, and overall appearance.

Grouping and Aligning Shapes and SmartArt

1. Grouping Shapes:

- To group multiple shapes together so they can be moved and formatted as a single unit, select all the shapes by holding down the Ctrl key and clicking on each shape.
- Right-click and choose **Group > Group.**

2. Aligning Shapes:

- Select the shapes you want to align. Go to the **Format** (or **Shape Format**) tab.
- Use the **Align** and **Distribute** options in the **Arrange** group to align shapes vertically or horizontally, distribute them evenly, or align them to the page.

Adding Alt Text for Accessibility

1. Alt Text for Shapes and SmartArt:

- Right-click on a shape or SmartArt graphic and select **Edit Alt Text.**

- In the **Alt Text** pane, provide a brief, descriptive title and description. This helps users with visual impairments understand the content of the graphic.

Saving and Reusing Shapes and SmartArt

1. Saving Shapes:

- Once you've customized a shape or group of shapes, you can save it as a **Shape** to reuse in other documents.

- Right-click on the shape or group, choose **Save as Picture**, and save it to your desired location.

2. Saving SmartArt Graphics:

- If you've customized a SmartArt graphic and want to reuse it, right-click on the SmartArt graphic and select **Save as Picture.**

Printing and Exporting

1. Printing:

- To print your document with shapes and SmartArt, go to **File > Print** and adjust print settings as needed.

2. Exporting as PDF or Image:

- If you need to share your document with others who may not have Word, consider exporting it as a PDF or image file.

- **Go to File > Save As** and choose **PDF** or **Image** format from the **Save as type** dropdown menu.

By incorporating shapes and SmartArt graphics into your Microsoft Word documents, you can effectively illustrate concepts, processes, hierarchies, and relationships, making your documents more engaging and informative.

Creating and Formatting Tables

Creating and Formatting Tables in Microsoft Word

Tables are powerful tools for organizing and presenting data in a structured format. Microsoft Word offers robust features for creating, customizing, and formatting tables to suit your document's needs.

Creating Tables

1. Inserting a Basic Table:
   - Place your cursor where you want to insert the table.
   - Go to the **Insert** tab.
   - Click the **Table** button in the **Tables** group.
   - Drag to select the number of rows and columns you want, or click **Insert Table** and specify the number of rows and columns.

2. Drawing a Custom Table:

- If you need a table with irregular row and column configurations, click the **Table** button and choose **Draw Table.**

- Use the pencil tool to draw the table grid manually.

3. Quick Tables:

- Click the **Table** button and select **Quick Tables** to choose from a gallery of preformatted table templates.

Adding and Deleting Rows and Columns

1. Adding Rows and Columns:

- To add a row or column, click in a cell next to where you want the new row or column to appear.

- Go to the **Layout** tab under **Table Tools.**

- In the **Rows & Columns** group, use **Insert Above, Insert Below, Insert Left,** or **Insert Right** to add a new row or column.

2. Deleting Rows and Columns:

- To delete a row or column, click in the row or column you want to delete.

- In the **Layout** tab under **Table Tools,** click **Delete** in the **Rows & Columns** group, then choose **Delete Row** or **Delete Column.**

Merging and Splitting Cells

1. Merging Cells:
- Select the cells you want to merge.
- Go to the **Layout** tab under **Table Tools.**
- Click **Merge Cells** in the **Merge** group.

2. Splitting Cells:
- Select the cell you want to split.
- In the **Layout** tab under **Table Tools,** click **Split Cells** in the **Merge** group.
- Specify the number of columns and rows into which you want to split the cell.

Formatting Tables

1. Applying Table Styles:
- Click anywhere in the table to select it.
- Go to the **Design** tab under **Table Tools.**

- In the **Table Styles** group, choose a preformatted style from the gallery. Use the **More** button to see additional styles.

2. Customizing Table Borders and Shading:

- To customize borders, go to the **Design** tab under **Table Tools.**
- Use the **Borders** button in the **Borders** group to apply or remove borders.
- To apply shading, click the **Shading** button in the **Table Styles** group and choose a color.

3. Adjusting Cell Size and Alignment:

- Select the cells you want to adjust.
- In the **Layout** tab under **Table Tools,** use the **Cell Size** group to adjust the height and width of cells.
- Use the **Alignment** group to change the alignment of text within the cells.

Sorting and Calculating Data

1. Sorting Data:

- Select the table or the columns you want to sort.

- Go to the **Layout** tab under **Table Tools.**

- Click **Sort** in the **Data** group and choose your sorting options.

2. Performing Calculations:

- Click in the cell where you want to insert the calculation.

- In the **Layout** tab under **Table Tools,** click **Formula** in the **Data** group.

- Enter the formula (e.g., =SUM(ABOVE)) and click **OK**.

Converting Text to Table and Table to Text

1. Converting Text to Table:

- Select the text you want to convert to a table.

- Go to the **Insert** tab, click **Table**, and choose **Convert Text to Table**.

- Specify the number of columns, rows, and how text is separated (e.g., by commas or tabs).

2. Converting Table to Text:

- Select the table you want to convert.

- In the **Layout** tab under **Table Tools,** click **Convert to Text** in the **Data** group.

- Choose how you want the table to be separated (e.g., tabs, commas) and click **OK.**

Using Table Properties

1. Accessing Table Properties:

- Right-click on the table and select **Table Properties**.

- Use the **Table Properties** dialog box to adjust the overall table alignment, row and column settings, and cell options.

2. Adjusting Row Height and Column Width:

- In the **Row** and **Column** tabs, set specific heights and widths or allow them to adjust automatically.

3. Cell Margins and Alignment:

- In the **Cell** tab, adjust cell margins and alignment to control how content is displayed within cells.

Working with Large Tables

1. Repeating Header Rows:

- For large tables that span multiple pages, repeat header rows at the top of each page.

- Select the header row, go to the **Layout** tab under **Table Tools,** and click **Repeat Header Rows** in the **Data** group.

2. Splitting a Table:

- Place the cursor where you want to split the table.

- In the **Layout** tab under **Table Tools,** click **Split Table** in the **Merge** group.

By mastering these table creation and formatting techniques, you can efficiently organize and present data in your Microsoft Word documents, ensuring a professional and polished appearance.

Using Charts and Graphs

Charts and graphs are powerful tools for visually representing data, making it easier to understand

and analyze information. Microsoft Word provides several options for inserting and customizing charts and graphs.

How you can effectively use them in your documents:

Inserting Charts and Graphs

1. Inserting a Chart:
   - Place your cursor where you want to insert the chart.
   - Go to the **Insert** tab.
   - Click the **Chart** button in the **Illustrations** group.
   - In the **Insert Chart** dialog box, select the type of chart you want (e.g., Column, Line, Pie, Bar, Area, Scatter) and click **OK**.
   - A placeholder chart will be inserted into your document, and an Excel window will open to input your data.

2. Entering Data for the Chart:

- In the Excel window that appears, enter your data in the provided cells.

- The chart in your Word document will update automatically to reflect the data you enter.

- Once you're done, close the Excel window.

Customizing Charts

1. Selecting the Chart:

- Click on the chart in your document to select it. This will display the **Chart Tools tabs: Design, Format,** and **Chart Elements**.

2. Changing the Chart Type:

- In the **Chart Tools Design** tab, click **Change Chart Type** in the **Type** group.

- Select a different chart type from the **Change Chart Type** dialog box and click **OK**.

3. Formatting Chart Elements:

- Click on individual elements of the chart (e.g., title, axis labels, legend) to select and format them.

- Use the **Format** tab under **Chart Tools** to change the fill color, outline, effects, and more.

4. Adding and Removing Chart Elements:

- In the **Chart Tools Design** tab, click **Add Chart Element** in the **Chart Layouts** group.

- You can add or remove elements such as titles, labels, gridlines, and legends.

- Alternatively, use the **Chart Elements** button (plus icon) that appears next to the chart when selected.

5. Applying Chart Styles:

- In the **Chart Tools Design** tab, use the **Chart Styles** group to quickly apply predefined styles and color schemes to your chart.

6. Customizing Data Labels:

- Click on the chart to select it.

- Go to the **Chart Tools Design** tab and click **Add Chart Element > Data Labels** to add labels to your data points.

- Choose the position for the labels (e.g., center, inside end, outside end).

Editing Chart Data

1. Editing Chart Data:

- To edit the data of an existing chart, click the chart to select it.

- In the **Chart Tools Design** tab, click **Edit Data** in the **Data** group.

- An Excel window will open where you can update your data. The chart in Word will automatically update to reflect the changes.

Working with Different Chart Types

1. Column and Bar Charts:

- Use these charts to compare values across categories. They are useful for showing changes over time or comparisons among items.

2. Line Charts:

- Line charts are ideal for showing trends over time. They are particularly useful for time-series data.

3. Pie Charts:

- Pie charts are used to show proportions of a whole. Each slice represents a category's contribution to the total.

4. Area Charts:

- Area charts are similar to line charts but with the area below the line filled in. They are useful for showing cumulative totals over time.

5. Scatter Charts:

- Scatter charts are used to show relationships between two variables. They are useful for identifying patterns and correlations.

Exporting and Printing Charts

1. Exporting Charts:

- To export a chart as an image, right-click the chart and select **Save as Picture.** Choose the desired file format and save it to your computer.

2. Printing Documents with Charts:

- Ensure your charts are correctly positioned and formatted before printing.

- Go to **File > Print** and adjust print settings as needed.

By effectively using charts and graphs in Microsoft Word, you can present data in a clear, visual manner, making your documents more informative and engaging.

Chapter 4: Advanced Features

Microsoft Word offers a plethora of advanced features that go beyond basic word processing, enabling users to create sophisticated documents with complex layouts, interactive elements, and streamlined workflows.

The overview of some of the most powerful advanced features in Word:

Using Macros

1. What are Macros?

- Macros are automated sequences of actions that you can record and playback to save time on repetitive tasks.

2. Recording a Macro:

- Go to the **View** tab.

- Click on **Macros** in the **Macros** group, then select **Record Macro**.

- Name your macro, assign a button or keyboard shortcut if desired, and choose where to store it (in the current document or all documents).

- Perform the actions you want to automate. When finished, go back to **View > Macros > Stop Recording.**

3. Running a Macro:

- To run a macro, go to **View > Macros > View Macros.**

- Select the macro you want to run and click **Run.**

Using Templates

1. What are Templates?

- Templates are pre-designed document formats that provide a consistent layout and design for various types of documents.

2. Using Built-in Templates:

- **Go to File > New.**

- Browse through the available templates, or use the search bar to find a specific template type.

- Click on a template to preview it, then click **Create** to use it.

3. Creating Custom Templates:

- Design your document with the desired layout and formatting.
- Go to **File > Save As.**
- Choose **Word Template (.dotx)** from the **Save as type** dropdown menu.
- Save the template to the desired location.

Collaborating with Others

1. Real-time Collaboration:

- Share your document with others by going to **File > Share > Share with People.**
- Enter the email addresses of your collaborators and choose their permission levels (can edit, can view).
- Collaborators can open the document and edit it simultaneously. Changes are updated in real-time.

2. Using Comments and Track Changes:

- Add comments to a document by selecting text and clicking **Review > New Comment.**

- Turn on **Track Changes** in the **Review** tab to keep track of all edits made to the document.

- Accept or reject changes by clicking **Review > Accept or Reject.**

Creating Forms

1. Inserting Form Controls:

- Go to the **Developer** tab (enable it from **File > Options > Customize Ribbon** if it's not visible).

- Use the **Controls** group to insert form elements like text boxes, checkboxes, drop-down lists, and more.

2. Protecting Forms:

- Once your form is created, you can restrict editing to just the form fields.

- Go to **Developer > Restrict Editing.**

- Check **Allow only this type of editing in the document,** select **Filling in forms,** and click **Yes, Start Enforcing Protection.**

Automating with Mail Merge

1. What is Mail Merge?
- Mail Merge allows you to create personalized documents, such as letters, emails, labels, or envelopes, by combining a template with a data source.

2. Setting Up Mail Merge:
- Go to the **Mailings** tab and click **Start Mail Merge.**
- Choose the type of document you want to create (e.g., letters, emails).
- Click **Select Recipients** and choose your data source (Excel, Outlook Contacts, or a new list).

3. Inserting Merge Fields:
- Click **Insert Merge Field** to add fields from your data source to the document.
- Format the document as needed.

4. Completing the Merge:

- Click **Finish & Merge** and choose how to complete the merge (e.g., print documents, send email messages).

Using References and Citations

1. Inserting Citations:
- Go to the **References** tab.
- Click **Insert Citation** and choose **Add New Source.**
- Enter the bibliographic information for your source.

2. Creating a Bibliography:
- Place your cursor where you want to insert the bibliography.
- Go to **References > Bibliography** and choose a style.

3. Adding Cross-references:
- Select the text or item you want to reference.
- Go to **References > Cross-reference.**
- Choose the reference type (e.g., heading, figure) and insert it.

Customizing the Ribbon and Quick Access Toolbar

1. Customizing the Ribbon:
  - Go to **File > Options > Customize Ribbon.**
  - Add, remove, or rearrange tabs and groups as needed.

2. Customizing the Quick Access Toolbar:
  - Click the drop-down arrow at the end of the Quick Access Toolbar.
  - Choose **More Commands** to add or remove commands.

By leveraging these advanced features in Microsoft Word, you can enhance your productivity, streamline your workflows, and create highly professional and customized documents.

Using Templates

Templates are a great way to save time and ensure consistency in your documents. Microsoft Word offers a variety of built-in templates for different types of documents, and you can also create your own custom templates to suit your specific needs.

How you can effectively use templates in Word:

Using Built-in Templates

1. Accessing Built-in Templates:
- Open Microsoft Word.
- Go to **File > New.**
- You will see a selection of featured templates, including templates for letters, resumes, flyers, calendars, and more.

2. Browsing and Searching for Templates:
- You can browse through different categories of templates by clicking on the category names.
- Use the search bar at the top to search for specific types of templates, such as "invoice," "brochure," or "newsletter."

3. Creating a Document from a Template:
- Click on a template to preview it.

- If the template meets your needs, click **Create** to open a new document based on the template.

- The template will open with predefined formatting and placeholder text, which you can replace with your own content.

Customizing Built-in Templates

1. Editing the Template:

- Once you have created a document from a template, you can customize it to better suit your needs.

- Modify the text, fonts, colors, and layout as required.

- Add or remove elements such as images, charts, and tables.

2. Saving the Customized Document:

- After making changes, you can save the document as a regular Word document by going to **File > Save As** and choosing a location and file name.

3. Saving the Customized Template:

- If you plan to use the customized layout frequently, save it as a new template.

- Go to **File > Save As.**

- Choose **Word Template (.dotx)** from the **Save as type** dropdown menu.

- Save the template to the desired location.

Creating Custom Templates

1. Designing Your Template:

- Start with a blank document or modify an existing document to create the layout and formatting you want for your template.

- Include any standard text, images, headers, footers, styles, and formatting that you want to be part of the template.

2. Saving as a Template:

- Once you have designed your template, save it by going to **File > Save As.**

- Choose **Word Template (.dotx)** from the **Save as type** dropdown menu.

- Save the template in the default template location or a folder of your choice.

3. Using Your Custom Template:

- To create a new document based on your custom template, go to **File > New.**

- Click **Personal** or **Custom** to access your saved templates.

- Select your custom template and click **Create.**

Managing Templates

1. Organizing Templates:

- Keep your templates organized by saving them in specific folders and naming them clearly.

- You can create subfolders within the default template folder to categorize templates by type or project.

2. Updating Templates:

- If you need to update a template, open it like a regular document, make the necessary changes, and save it again as a template.

- Ensure that you replace the old version or save the updated version with a new name.

3. Deleting Templates:

- To delete a template, navigate to the folder where your templates are saved.

- Select the template file and delete it like any other file.

Sharing Templates

1. Sharing Templates with Others:

- To share a template with others, send the template file **(.dotx)** via email or share it through a cloud storage service like OneDrive or Google Drive.

- Ensure that the recipients save the template in their template folder for easy access.

2. Using Shared Templates:

- If you receive a template from someone else, save it to your template folder.

- Access the shared template by going to **File > New > Personal or Custom.**

By effectively applying and managing templates in Microsoft Word, you can streamline your document creation process, maintain consistency in formatting, and save time on repetitive tasks. Templates are particularly useful for businesses and individuals who need to create multiple documents with a similar structure and design.

Working with Headers and Footers

Headers and footers are sections at the top and bottom of each page in a document. They can include text, graphics, page numbers, the date, the document title, and other information. Using headers and footers can enhance the organization and appearance of your documents.

Here's how to effectively work with headers and footers in Microsoft Word:

Inserting Headers and Footers

1. Inserting a Header or Footer:
   - Go to the **Insert** tab.

- In the **Header & Footer** group, click either **Header** or **Footer**.

- Choose from a gallery of built-in styles or select **Edit Header** or **Edit Footer** to create a custom header or footer.

2. Editing a Header or Footer:

- Once the header or footer area is open, you can type and format text as you would in the main document.

- Use the **Header & Footer Tools Design** tab to add elements like page numbers, date and time, document title, or other information.

Adding Page Numbers

1. Inserting Page Numbers:

- Go to the **Insert** tab.

- Click **Page Number** in the **Header & Footer** group.

- Choose where you want the page numbers to appear (top of the page, bottom of the page, etc.) and select a specific style.

2. Customizing Page Numbers:

- To format page numbers, click **Page Number** and then **Format Page Numbers.**

- In the dialog box, you can choose the number format, start at a specific number, or include chapter numbers.

Different First Page and Odd/Even Pages

1. Different First Page:

- If you want a different header or footer for the first page (e.g., no header on the title page), go to the **Header & Footer Tools Design** tab.

- Check the **Different First Page** box. Customize the first page header or footer as needed.

2. Different Odd and Even Pages:

- For different headers and footers on odd and even pages (useful for books and manuals), check the **Different Odd & Even Pages** box in the **Header & Footer Tools Design** tab.

- Customize the headers and footers for odd and even pages accordingly.

Using Section Breaks

1. Creating Sections with Different Headers and Footers:

- Insert a section break where you want to change the header or footer. Go to the **Layout** tab, click **Breaks** in the **Page Setup** group, and select the appropriate section break **(e.g., Next Page).**

- Each section can have its own headers and footers. To unlink the header or footer from the previous section, go to the **Header & Footer Tools Design** tab and click **Link to Previous** to turn it off.

2. Editing Headers and Footers in Different Sections:

- Navigate to the header or footer in the new section.

- Customize the header or footer for the new section without affecting previous sections.

Adding Graphics to Headers and Footers

1. Inserting Images:

- Click inside the header or footer area.

- Go to the **Insert** tab and click **Pictures** or **Online Pictures** to insert an image.

- Resize and position the image as needed.

2. Adding Shapes or Lines:

- Click inside the header or footer area.

- Go to the **Insert** tab and click **Shapes** to insert lines, rectangles, or other shapes.

- Draw and format the shapes as needed.

Advanced Header and Footer Options

1. Using Document Information:

- Use the **Quick Parts** feature to insert document properties like the author's name, document title, or file path. Go to **Insert > Quick Parts > Field** and choose the desired property.

2. Adding Dynamic Content:

- Insert fields that automatically update, such as the current date or total number of pages. Go to **Insert > Quick Parts > Field,** then select and customize the field.

3. Linking to Previous:

- By default, headers and footers in new sections are linked to the previous section. To customize headers or footers independently, go to the **Header & Footer Tools Design** tab and click **Link to Previous** to unlink them.

Removing Headers and Footers

1. Removing Headers and Footers from the Entire Document:

- Go to the **Inser** tab.
- Click **Heade** or **Footer** and then select **Remove Header** or **Remove Footer.**

2. Removing Headers and Footers from Specific Sections:

- Navigate to the section with the header or footer you want to remove.
- In the **Header & Footer Tools Design** tab, click **Header** or **Footer**, and select **Remove Header** or **Remove Footer.**

Mastering headers and footers in Microsoft Word, you can significantly enhance the professionalism and navigability of your documents. Whether you're working on academic papers, business reports, or creative projects, effective use of headers and footers can help you create polished, well-organized documents.

Inserting Page Numbers and Table of Contents

Adding page numbers and a table of contents can greatly enhance the organization and navigation of your document.

How you can insert and customize these elements in Microsoft Word:

Inserting Page Numbers

1. Inserting Basic Page Numbers:
   - Go to the **Insert** tab.

- In the **Header & Footer** group, click **Page Number**.

- Choose the location where you want the page numbers to appear (e.g., top of the page, bottom of the page).

- Select a specific style from the gallery.

2. Customizing Page Numbers:

- To format page numbers, click **Page Number** again, then select **Format Page Numbers.**

- In the **Page Number Format** dialog box, you can:

  - Choose a number format (e.g., 1, 2, 3 or i, ii, iii).

  - Set the starting page number.

  - Include chapter numbers if your document is divided into chapters.

3. Different First Page:

- If you want the first page to have no page number (common for title pages), go to the **Header & Footer Tools Design** tab.

- Check the **Different First Page** box. The first page will have a unique header/footer where you can leave out the page number.

4. Different Odd and Even Pages:
- For different headers and footers on odd and even pages (useful for books and manuals), check the **Different Odd & Even Pages** box in the **Header & Footer Tools Design** tab.
- Customize the headers and footers for odd and even pages accordingly.

5. Removing Page Numbers:
- To remove page numbers, go to the **Insert** tab.
- Click **Page Number,** then select **Remove Page Numbers.**

Inserting a Table of Contents

1. Preparing Your Document:
- Ensure your document is properly formatted with headings. Use Word's built-in heading styles (e.g., **Heading 1, Heading 2, Heading 3**).

- Apply these styles to the titles and subtitles you want to include in your table of contents.

2. Inserting the Table of Contents:
- Place your cursor where you want to insert the table of contents (usually at the beginning of the document).
- Go to the **References** tab.
- Click **Table of Contents** in the **Table of Contents** group.
- Choose an automatic table from the gallery. Word will generate a table of contents based on the heading styles used in your document.

3. Customizing the Table of Contents:
- To customize the appearance of the table of contents, click **Table of Contents** again, then select **Custom Table of Contents.**
- In the **Table of Contents** dialog box, you can:
  - Change the format and style.
  - Modify the number of heading levels included.
  - Adjust the tab leader (the characters that appear between the headings and page numbers).

4. Updating the Table of Contents:

- If you make changes to your document (e.g., add or remove sections), you'll need to update the table of contents.

- Click anywhere in the table of contents to select it.

- Click **Update Table** in the **Table of Contents** group on the **References** tab.

- Choose to update the entire table or just the page numbers.

5. Removing the Table of Contents:

- To remove the table of contents, go to the **References** tab.

- Click **Table of Contents,** then select **Remove Table of Contents.**

Tips for Effective Page Numbers and Table of Contents

- **Consistency:** Ensure that your heading styles are applied consistently throughout your document for an accurate table of contents.

- **Preview:** Use the print preview feature to see how your page numbers and table of contents will look when printed.

- **Section Breaks:** Use section breaks to manage different numbering schemes within the same document (e.g., Roman numerals for front matter and Arabic numerals for the main content).

- **Navigation:** The table of contents not only provides an overview of your document but also allows readers to quickly navigate to specific sections by holding the Ctrl key (Cmd key on Mac) and clicking on the entry.

By effectively using page numbers and a table of contents, you can improve the readability and professional appearance of your Microsoft Word documents.

Reviewing and Tracking Changes

Reviewing and tracking changes are essential features in Microsoft Word, especially when collaborating on documents. These tools allow multiple users to make edits, suggest revisions, and provide feedback while maintaining a clear record of all modifications.

How to effectively use these features:

Tracking Changes

1. Turning on Track Changes:
  - Go to the **Review** tab.
  - In the **Tracking** group, click **Track Changes**. This will highlight the button, indicating that the feature is enabled.

2. Customizing Track Changes:
  - Click the small arrow in the **Tracking** group to open the **Track Changes Options.**
  - In the **Advanced Track Changes Options,** you can customize how changes are displayed, including color coding for insertions, deletions, and formatting changes.

3. Viewing Changes:

- Use the **Display** for **Review** dropdown in the **Tracking** group to choose how you want to view the document:

- **Simple Markup:** Shows the final version with changes indicated by a red line in the margin.

- **All Markup:** Shows all changes and comments in the document.

- **No Markup:** Shows the final version without markup.

- **Original:** Shows the original version without any changes.

4. Navigating Changes:

- Use the **Previous** and **Next** buttons in the **Changes** group on the **Review** tab to navigate through the tracked changes.

Reviewing Changes

1. Accepting or Rejecting Changes:

- To accept or reject changes, click on the change to select it.

- In the **Changes** group on the **Review** tab, click **Accept** or **Reject**.

- Use the dropdown menus next to **Accept** and **Reject** to accept/reject all changes or only the selected change.

2. Using Comments:

- To add a comment, select the text you want to comment on.
- Click **New Comment** in the **Comments** group on the **Review** tab.
- Type your comment in the comment balloon that appears in the margin.

3. Replying to Comments:

- Click on an existing comment and select **Reply**. This allows you to respond directly to the comment within the same balloon.

4. Deleting Comments:

- Select the comment you want to delete.
- In the **Comments** group on the **Review** tab, click **Delete**.
- Use the dropdown menu to delete all comments or only the selected comment.

Comparing and Combining Documents

1. Comparing Documents:
- Go to the **Review** tab.
- In the **Compare** group, click **Compare**.
- Select **Compare** from the dropdown menu.
- Choose the original document and the revised document.
- Word will generate a new document showing the differences between the two.

2. Combining Documents:
- Go to the **Review** tab.
- In the **Compare** group, click **Compare**.
- Select **Combine** from the dropdown menu.
- Choose the original document and the revised document.
- Word will combine the documents and display all changes.

Protecting Documents for Review

1. Restricting Editing:
- Go to the **Review** tab.

- In the **Protect** group, click **Restrict Editing.**

- In the **Restrict Editing** pane, check **Allow only this type of editing in the document** and select **Tracked changes.**

- Click **Yes, Start Enforcing Protection** and set a password if desired.

2. Marking a Document as Final:

- Go to the **File** tab.

- Click **Info.**

- Click **Protect Document** and select **Mark as Final.** This makes the document read-only, indicating that it is the final version.

Reviewing Changes Efficiently

1. Using the Reviewing Pane:

- Open the **Reviewing Pane** by clicking **Reviewing Pane** in the **Tracking** group. This provides a summary of all tracked changes and comments in the document.

2. Filtering Changes:

- Use the **Show Markup** dropdown in the **Tracking** group to filter the types of changes and reviewers you want to see.

3. Managing Multiple Reviewers:

- Each reviewer's changes are marked with their name and a unique color, making it easy to identify who made each change.
- Use the **Reviewers** dropdown in the **Tracking** group to view or hide changes by specific reviewers.

mastering the review and track changes features in Microsoft Word, you can enhance collaboration, ensure accuracy, and streamline the editing process. These tools are invaluable for maintaining a clear and organized record of all changes and comments, making it easier to produce polished and professional documents.

Chapter 5: Finalizing and Sharing Your Document

After you've completed drafting and editing your document, the next steps involve finalizing and sharing it. This process ensures that your document is polished, professional, and ready for distribution.

Here's a comprehensive guide to finalizing and sharing your Microsoft Word document:

Reviewing Your Document

1. Proofreading:

   - Use the **Spelling & Grammar** tool to check for spelling and grammatical errors. Go to the **Review** tab and click **Spelling & Grammar** in the **Proofing** group.

   - Carefully read through the document to catch any errors or inconsistencies that the tool might have missed.

2. Using the Thesaurus:

- Enhance your writing by using the Thesaurus. Right-click on a word and select **Synonyms** to see a list of alternatives. You can also go to the **Review** tab and click **Thesaurus** in the **Proofing** group.

3. Checking Word Count:

- Ensure your document meets any word count requirements. Go to the **Review** tab and click **Word Count** in the **Proofing** group.

Formatting Your Document

1. Applying Consistent Styles:

- Ensure that your document has a consistent look by applying styles to headings, paragraphs, and other text elements. Go to the **Home** tab and use the **Styles** group to apply predefined styles.

2. Using the Format Painter:

- Quickly copy formatting from one part of your document to another using the **Format Painter**. Select the formatted text, click the **Format Painter** in the **Clipboard** group on the **Home** tab, and then apply it to the target text.

3. Adjusting Page Layout:

- Check the overall layout of your document. Go to the **Layout** tab to adjust margins, orientation, size, and columns.

4. Inserting a Table of Contents:

- If your document is long or complex, consider adding a table of contents. Go to the **References** tab and click **Table of Contents** in the **Table of Contents** group. Select an automatic table from the gallery.

Inspecting the Document

1. Using the Document Inspector:

- Before sharing your document, use the Document Inspector to check for hidden metadata or personal information. Go to the **File** tab, click **Info**, select **Check for Issues,** and choose **Inspect Document.**

2. Removing Personal Information:

- The Document Inspector can remove personal information and hidden data. After running the inspection, choose to remove all found items to ensure privacy.

3. Accessibility Check:

- Ensure your document is accessible to all readers by running an accessibility check. Go to the **Review** tab, click **Check Accessibility** in the **Accessibility** group, and follow the recommendations.

Saving and Exporting

1. Saving in Different Formats:

- Save your document in various formats depending on your needs. Go to the **File** tab, click **Save As,** and choose from options like Word Document **(.docx)**, PDF **(.pdf)**, or Web Page **(.html)**.

2. Password Protection:

- Protect sensitive information by adding a password to your document. Go to the **File** tab, click **Info**, select **Protect Document,** and choose **Encrypt with Password.**

3. Creating a Read-Only Version:
- To prevent further editing, save your document as a read-only file. Go to the **File** tab, click **Save As,** and select **Tools > General Options.** Check the **Read-only recommended** box and save.

Sharing Your Document

1. Emailing Directly from Word:
- You can email your document directly from Word. Go to the **File** tab, click **Share,** and select **Email**. Choose to send the document as an attachment, PDF, or XPS.

2. Using OneDrive:
- Share your document using OneDrive for easy collaboration. Go to the **File** tab, click **Share,** and select **Save to Cloud.** Upload your document to

OneDrive, then choose **Share** to invite others to view or edit.

3. Collaborating in Real-Time:

- For real-time collaboration, save your document to OneDrive or SharePoint. Go to the **File** tab, click **Share**, and select **Share with People.** Invite collaborators by entering their email addresses and assigning permissions (can edit or can view).

4. Publishing Online:

- Publish your document online for broader access. Go to the **File** tab, click **Share,** and select **Post to Blog** or **Present Online.**

Final Checks

1. Previewing Your Document:

- Preview your document before finalizing it. Go to the **File** tab, click **Print**, and use the print preview to see how the document will look on paper.

2. Printing:

- If you need physical copies, print your document. Go to the **File** tab, click **Print,** and select your printer and print settings.

By following these steps, you can ensure that your Microsoft Word document is thoroughly reviewed, properly formatted, and securely shared. This process not only enhances the professionalism of your work but also makes it accessible and ready for distribution to your intended audience.

Proofreading Tools

Proofreading Tools in Microsoft Word

Proofreading is an essential step in finalizing any document, ensuring that your writing is clear, error-free, and professional. Microsoft Word offers a variety of built-in tools to help you proofread your document effectively.

How to make the most of these proofreading tools:

Spelling and Grammar Check

1. Automatic Spelling and Grammar Check:

- Microsoft Word automatically checks for spelling and grammar errors as you type. Spelling errors are underlined in red, and grammar errors are underlined in blue.

- Right-click on the underlined word or phrase to see suggestions and choose the appropriate correction.

2. Running a Full Spelling and Grammar Check:

- Go to the **Review** tab.

- In the **Proofing** group, click **Spelling & Grammar**.

- Word will review your document and provide suggestions for corrections. You can choose to accept or ignore each suggestion.

3. Customizing the Spelling and Grammar Settings:

- Go to **File** > **Options** > **Proofing.**

- Customize your preferences for spelling and grammar checks, such as adding words to the custom dictionary or adjusting grammar settings.

Thesaurus

1. Using the Thesaurus:

- Enhance your writing by finding synonyms for overused or repetitive words.
- Right-click on a word and select **Synonyms** to see a list of alternatives.
- Alternatively, go to the **Review** tab and click **Thesaurus** in the **Proofing** group. A pane will open on the right side with synonym suggestions.

Readability Statistics

1. Enabling Readability Statistics:

- Go to **File** > **Options** > **Proofing**.
- Under **When correcting spelling and grammar in Word,** check **Show readability statistics.**
- After running a full spelling and grammar check, Word will display readability statistics, including the

Flesch Reading Ease score and the Flesch-Kincaid Grade Level.

2. Interpreting Readability Statistics:

- The Flesch Reading Ease score indicates how easy your text is to read. Higher scores suggest easier readability.

- The Flesch-Kincaid Grade Level indicates the U.S. school grade level needed to understand the text. Lower scores suggest simpler text.

Language Preferences

1. Setting the Document Language:

- Go to the **Review** tab.

- In the **Language** group, click **Language** and select **Set Proofing Language**.

- Choose the desired language for spelling and grammar checks.

2. Adding Proofing Tools for Additional Languages:

- If you need to proofread in multiple languages, you can add proofing tools for additional languages.

- Go to **File** > **Options** > **Language**.

- Under **Choose Editing Languages,** add the languages you need. Word will download the necessary proofing tools.

AutoCorrect and AutoFormat

1. Using AutoCorrect:

- Word automatically corrects common spelling and typing errors using the AutoCorrect feature.

- Go to **File** > **Options** > **Proofing** > **AutoCorrect Options** to view and customize the list of AutoCorrect entries.

2. Customizing AutoCorrect Entries:

- Add your own AutoCorrect entries for frequently mistyped words or phrases.

- In the **AutoCorrect Options** dialog box, enter the incorrect text in the **Replace** field and the correct text in the **With** field.

Comments and Suggestions

1. Adding Comments:

- Use comments to make notes or suggest changes without altering the text.

- Select the text you want to comment on, go to the **Review** tab, and click **New Comment** in the **Comments** group.

- Type your comment in the comment balloon that appears.

2. Reviewing Comments:

- Navigate through comments using the **Previous** and **Next** buttons in the **Comments** group on the **Review** tab.

- Reply to or delete comments as needed.

Reviewing Pane

1. Using the Reviewing Pane:

- The Reviewing Pane provides a summary of all tracked changes and comments.

- Go to the **Review** tab and click **Reviewing Pane** in the **Tracking** group.

- Choose to display the pane vertically or horizontally. This helps you see an overview of all edits and comments in your document.

Additional Proofreading Tips

1. Read Aloud:

- Use the **Read Aloud** feature to have Word read your document to you. Hearing your text can help you catch errors you might miss when reading silently.

- Go to the **Review** tab and click **Read Aloud** in the **Speech** group.

2. Take Breaks:

- Proofread your document in stages. Take breaks to rest your eyes and return with a fresh perspective.

3. Print and Proofread:

- Sometimes, it's easier to spot errors on a printed copy. Print your document and review it carefully.

By utilizing these proofreading tools in Microsoft Word, you can ensure that your document is polished, error-free, and ready for sharing or publication.

Printing Options

Printing Options in Microsoft Word

Printing your document is often the final step before distribution or archiving. Microsoft Word provides various printing options to ensure your document is printed correctly and efficiently. Here's how to navigate the printing process and utilize different printing options:

Accessing Printing Options

1. Opening the Print Dialog:
   - Go to the **File** tab.
   - Click **Print** in the left-hand menu. Alternatively, use the shortcut **Ctrl + P.**

2. Navigating the Print Dialog:

- The Print dialog box allows you to set printing preferences and preview your document before printing.

Basic Printing Settings

1. Printer Selection:
- Choose the printer you want to use from the **Printer** dropdown menu.
- If your printer is connected to a network or shared, ensure it's selected correctly.

2. Number of Copies:
- Specify the number of copies you want to print using the **Copies** field.

3. Page Range:
  - **Select which pages to print:**
    - **All:** Print the entire document.
    - **Current Page:** Print only the page currently displayed.
    - **Pages:** Specify a range of pages to print (e.g., 1-3, 5, 7).

Page Setup Options

1. Paper Size:
- Choose the size of paper to print on (e.g., Letter, A4, Legal) from the **Paper Size** dropdown menu.

2. Orientation:
- Select **Portrait** (vertical) or **Landscape** (horizontal) orientation for printing.

3. Margins:
- Adjust the margins of your document using the **Margins** dropdown menu or by clicking **Margins** and selecting **Custom Margins** for more precise adjustments.

4. Scaling:
- Use the **Scaling** options to adjust the size of the document on the page:
  - **No Scaling:** Print at the document's actual size.
  - **Fit to:** Scale the document to fit a specific number of pages wide and tall.

- **Custom Scale:** Enter a percentage to scale the document size.

Print Preview

1. Previewing Your Document:
- Before printing, click **Print Preview** to see how your document will look when printed.
- Use the navigation buttons to view different pages and ensure everything appears as expected.

2. Adjusting Print Settings from Print Preview:
- Click **Settings** to adjust printer-specific settings and preferences directly from the Print Preview screen.

Advanced Printing Options

1. Print Quality:
- Choose the print quality or resolution from the **Print Quality** dropdown menu. Options may include Draft, Normal, or Best.

2. Duplex Printing:

- If your printer supports duplex (double-sided) printing, choose **Print on Both Sides** to print on both sides of the paper automatically.

3. Color or Black and White:

- Select whether to print in **Color** or **Black and White** depending on your document and printer capabilities.

4. Watermark and Backgrounds:

- Include or exclude document watermarks and backgrounds from the **Options** section of the Print dialog box.

Saving as PDF or XPS

1. Creating a PDF:

- Instead of printing to paper, save your document as a PDF file. This is useful for electronic distribution or archiving.
- Go to the **File** tab, click **Save As,** and choose **PDF (.pdf)** from the **Save as type** dropdown menu.

2. Saving as XPS:

- Similar to saving as PDF, you can save your document as an XPS file (XML Paper Specification) for electronic distribution or archiving.

- Go to the **File** tab, click **Save As,** and choose **XPS Document (.xps)** from the **Save as type** dropdown menu.

Final Steps

1. Printing Your Document:

- Once you've configured your printing options, click **Print** in the Print dialog box to send your document to the printer.

2. Checking Printer Status:

- Monitor the printer status from the notification area or printer software to ensure your document prints successfully.

By utilizing these printing options in Microsoft Word, you can efficiently produce printed copies or electronic versions of your documents while ensuring they meet your desired specifications and quality standards.

Exporting and Sharing Documents

Exporting and Sharing Documents from Microsoft Word

Exporting and sharing your Microsoft Word documents allows you to distribute them electronically, collaborate with others, or prepare them for different uses. Here's a guide on how to export and share documents effectively:

Saving Your Document

1. Saving in Different Formats:
   - Go to the **File** tab.
   - Click **Save As** to save your document in a different format than the default .docx.
   - Choose from formats like:
   - **PDF (.pdf):** Ideal for sharing documents that retain formatting across different devices.

- XPS Document (.xps): An alternative to PDF for electronic distribution or archiving.

- Web Page (.htm; .html): Converts your document into a web page format for online viewing.

- Plain Text (.txt): Saves your document as plain text without any formatting.

2. Compatibility Mode:

- If you need to save in an older Word format for compatibility with previous versions of Word, choose **Word 97-2003 Document (.doc)** from the **Save as type** dropdown menu.

Sharing Options

1. Emailing Your Document:

- Go to the **File** tab.
- Click **Share** and select **Email**. Choose **Send as Attachment, PDF, or XPS** depending on your needs.
- Alternatively, save your document and attach it to an email manually.

2. Saving to OneDrive or SharePoint:

- Save your document to Microsoft OneDrive or SharePoint for easy sharing and collaboration.

- Click **Save As** > **OneDrive - Personal** or **OneDrive - Company Name** (if connected to a SharePoint account).

3. Sharing a Link:

- After saving to OneDrive or SharePoint, click **Share** in the **File** tab.

- Enter email addresses of recipients to grant them access to view or edit the document.

- Choose whether recipients can edit or only view the document.

Collaboration and Real-Time Editing

1. Real-Time Collaboration:

- Save your document to OneDrive or SharePoint.

- Click **Share** and invite others to edit the document simultaneously.

- Changes are automatically synced across all devices, facilitating real-time collaboration.

2. Tracking Changes:

- Use the **Track Changes** feature to keep track of edits made by different users.

- Go to the **Review** tab, click **Track Changes,** and choose **All Markup** to show all changes made to the document.

Final Steps

1. Printing:

- If you need physical copies, go to the **File** tab, click **Print,** And configure your printing options as needed. See earlier responses for more details.

2. Securing Your Document:

- Protect sensitive information by adding passwords to your document.

- Go to the **File** tab, click **Info,** select **Protect Document,** and choose **Encrypt with Password.**

3. Final Review:

- Before sharing or distributing your document, perform a final review to ensure all content, formatting, and security settings are correct.

Additional Tips

1. Version Control:

- Use file naming conventions or version control tools to keep track of different iterations of your document.

- For example, append version numbers or dates to the file name (e.g., Document_v1.0.docx, Document_July2024.docx).

2. Data Privacy:

- Be mindful of data privacy regulations when sharing documents containing sensitive information.

- Avoid sharing via insecure channels or with unauthorized recipients.

By following these steps and utilizing the export and sharing options in Microsoft Word, you can efficiently distribute your documents, collaborate effectively, and ensure your content reaches the intended audience in the desired format.

Collaborating with Others

Collaborating with others on Microsoft Word documents allows multiple users to work together on the same document, make edits, and provide feedback.

Comprehensive guide on how to collaborate effectively using Microsoft Word:

Setting Up Collaboration

1. Save to OneDrive or SharePoint:
  - **OneDrive:** For personal use and small teams.
  - **SharePoint:** Ideal for larger teams within an organization, offering more robust collaboration features.

2. Sharing Your Document:
  - Go to the **File** tab.
  - Click **Share** and select **Save to Cloud.**
  - Choose **OneDrive** or **SharePoint** and follow prompts to save the document.

Real-Time Collaboration

1. Inviting Collaborators:

 - After saving to OneDrive or SharePoint, click **Share** again.

 - Enter the email addresses of collaborators.

 - Choose whether they can **Edit** or **View** the document.

2. Simultaneous Editing:

 - Collaborators can edit the document simultaneously.

 - Changes are synced in real-time, visible to all users.

Tracking Changes and Comments

1. Track Changes:

 - Go to the **Review** tab.

 - Click **Track Changes** to enable.

 - Edits appear marked with each collaborator's name and color.

2. Adding Comments:

- Select text, go to **Review** tab, click **New Comment.**

- Type feedback or questions for collaborators.

Reviewing Edits

1. Accepting or Rejecting Changes:

- In the **Review** tab, use **Accept** or **Reject** to manage edits.

- Choose to apply changes individually or collectively.

2. Navigating Changes:

- Use **Previous** and **Next** in the **Changes** group to move between edits.

Communication

1. Chat and Collaboration:

- Utilize built-in chat features or external communication tools to discuss changes.

- Keep communication organized and relevant to the document.

Security and Permissions

1. Managing Permissions:

- Control who can access or edit the document.

- Adjust permissions via OneDrive or SharePoint settings.

Finalizing Collaboration

1. Review and Proofread:

- After edits, perform a final review.

- Use proofreading tools to check for errors.

2. Saving and Distributing:

- Save the final document.

- Share via email, download, or print as needed.

Tips for Effective Collaboration

1. Clear Communication:

- Communicate goals, expectations, and deadlines clearly.

2. Version Control:

- Use version history in OneDrive or SharePoint to track changes.

3. Document Management:
- Keep files organized and labeled for easy reference.

4. Training and Support:
- Provide training on collaboration tools for all team members.

By following these steps, you can leverage Microsoft Word's collaboration features to work efficiently with others, streamline document creation, and ensure accuracy and professionalism in your shared documents.

Appendix: Additional Tips and Tricks

Additional Tips and Tricks for Microsoft Word

Mastering Microsoft Word involves not only knowing its basic functions but also leveraging various tips and tricks to enhance productivity and efficiency. Here are some advanced tips and tricks to help you make the most out of Microsoft Word:

Formatting Tips

1. Quick Styles: Use Quick Styles to quickly apply consistent formatting across headings, paragraphs, and other text elements. Customize styles in the Styles gallery to match your document's aesthetic.

2. Format Painter: Easily copy formatting from one part of your document to another using the Format Painter tool. Select formatted text, click Format Painter on the Home tab, and then apply it to other text.

3. Keyboard Shortcuts: Learn and use keyboard shortcuts to speed up tasks. For example, **Ctrl + B** for bold, **Ctrl + I** for italic, **Ctrl + U** for underline, and **Ctrl + S** to save.

Productivity Enhancements

1. Navigation Pane: Use the Navigation Pane (View tab > Navigation Pane) to quickly navigate through headings and search for specific content within your document.

2. Split View: Split your document window (View tab > Split) to view different parts of your document simultaneously, making it easier to reference or edit content.

3. Document Map: Enable the Document Map (View tab > Document Views > Document Map) to see an overview of your document's structure and navigate quickly.

Editing and Reviewing

1. Track Changes: Use Track Changes (Review tab > Track Changes) to keep track of edits made by yourself and collaborators. Choose to accept or reject changes as needed.

2. Comments and Annotations: Use comments (Review tab > New Comment) to provide feedback or ask questions within the document. Reply to comments and resolve threads when issues are addressed.

3. Compare Documents: Compare two versions of a document to see the differences. Go to the Review tab, click Compare, and select Compare or Combine.

Efficiency Tools

1. AutoCorrect: Customize AutoCorrect options (File tab > Options > Proofing > AutoCorrect Options) to automatically correct common typos and format text as you type.

2. Building Blocks: Use Quick Parts and Building Blocks to insert reusable content such as cover pages, headers, footers, and text snippets. Manage and create your own Building Blocks Organizer.

3. Macros: Record and run macros (View tab > Macros) to automate repetitive tasks. Customize macros using Visual Basic for Applications (VBA) for more advanced automation.

Customization and Personalization

1. Custom Templates: Create and use custom templates (File tab > New > Personal) to standardize document formats and layouts for specific purposes or projects.

2. Custom Ribbon: Customize the Ribbon (File tab > Options > Customize Ribbon) to add frequently used commands or remove unused ones, optimizing your workflow.

Collaboration and Sharing

1. Cloud Integration: Save documents to OneDrive or SharePoint for easy sharing and collaboration. Access documents from multiple devices and enable real-time editing.

2. Version History: Use version history in OneDrive or SharePoint to view and restore previous versions of your document, tracking changes over time.

Security and Protection

1. Document Encryption: Protect sensitive documents by encrypting them with a password (File tab > Info > Protect Document > Encrypt with Password).

2. Document Properties: Review and update document properties (File tab > Info > Properties) such as title, author, and keywords for better organization and searchability.

Accessibility and Compliance

1. Accessibility Checker: Use the Accessibility Checker (Review tab > Check Accessibility) to ensure your document is accessible to users with disabilities. Follow recommendations to improve accessibility.

2. Document Compliance: Ensure your document meets regulatory compliance requirements by checking and addressing issues related to privacy, security, and document structure.

Finalizing and Printing

1. Print Options: Customize print settings (File tab > Print) such as page orientation, paper size, margins, and print quality. Preview your document before printing to ensure it appears as expected.

2. Saving as PDF or XPS: Save documents as PDF or XPS files (File tab > Save As) for easy distribution and viewing across different platforms while preserving formatting.

Continuous Learning

1. Online Resources: Explore online tutorials, forums, and Microsoft's official documentation for updates, tips, and advanced techniques in Microsoft Word.

2. Training Courses: Consider taking formal training courses or workshops to deepen your knowledge and skills in Microsoft Word.

Applying these tips and tricks into your workflow, you can enhance your productivity, streamline document creation and editing, collaborate effectively with others, and ensure your documents are professional and polished.

Keyboard Shortcuts

Mastering keyboard shortcuts can significantly enhance your productivity in Microsoft Word.

Here are some essential keyboard shortcuts to help you navigate, format, and work efficiently:

Navigation Shortcuts

1. **Ctrl + Home:** Move to the beginning of the document.
2. **Ctrl + End:** Move to the end of the document.
3. **Ctrl + Page Up:** Move to the top of the previous page.
4. **Ctrl + Page Down:** Move to the top of the next page.
5. **Ctrl + Left Arrow:** Move one word to the left.
6. **Ctrl + Right Arrow:** Move one word to the right.
7. **Ctrl + Up Arrow:** Move to the beginning of the previous paragraph.
8. **Ctrl + Down Arrow:** Move to the beginning of the next paragraph.
9. **Ctrl + G:** Go to a specific page, section, line, or bookmark.

Selection Shortcuts

1. **Shift + Arrow Keys:** Extend the selection one character or line at a time.

2. Ctrl + Shift + Left Arrow: Select the previous word.

3. Ctrl + Shift + Right Arrow: Select the next word.

4. Ctrl + Shift + Up Arrow: Select from the current cursor position to the beginning of the paragraph.

5. Ctrl + Shift + Down Arrow: Select from the current cursor position to the end of the paragraph.

6. Ctrl + A: Select the entire document.

Editing Shortcuts

1. Ctrl + X: Cut selected text or object.

2. Ctrl + C: Copy selected text or object.

3. Ctrl + V: Paste cut or copied text or object.

4. Ctrl + Z: Undo the last action.

5. Ctrl + Y: Redo the last undone action.

6. Ctrl + F: Open the Navigation pane to search within the document.

7. Ctrl + H: Open the Replace pane to find and replace text.

Formatting Shortcuts

1. **Ctrl + B:** Bold selected text.

2. **Ctrl + I:** Italicize selected text.

3. **Ctrl + U:** Underline selected text.

4. **Ctrl + E:** Center-align selected text.

5. **Ctrl + L:** Left-align selected text.

6. **Ctrl + R:** Right-align selected text.

7. **Ctrl + 1:** Set single-line spacing.

8. **Ctrl + 2:** Set double-line spacing.

9. **Ctrl + 5:** Set 1.5-line spacing.

Review and Navigation Shortcuts

1. **F7:** Run a spelling and grammar check.

2. **Alt + Shift + E:** Edit and move between comments in the document.

3. **Ctrl + Shift + E:** Track or turn off changes.

File and General Shortcuts

1. **Ctrl + S:** Save the document.

2. **Ctrl + N:** Create a new document.

3. **Ctrl + O:** Open an existing document.

4. **Ctrl + P:** Print the document.

Other Useful Shortcuts

1. **Ctrl + K:** Insert a hyperlink.
2. **Ctrl + Enter:** Insert a page break.
3. **Alt + Shift + D:** Insert the current date.
4. **Alt + Shift + T:** Insert the current time.

These keyboard shortcuts will help you navigate Microsoft Word more efficiently, streamline document creation and editing tasks, and improve your overall productivity. Practice using these shortcuts regularly to become more proficient and save time while working with Word documents.

Customizing the Ribbon and Quick Access Toolbar

Customizing the Ribbon and Quick Access Toolbar in Microsoft Word allows you to streamline your workflow by placing frequently used commands and tools within easy reach.

How you can customize these elements to suit your needs:

Customizing the Ribbon

1. Adding Commands to the Ribbon:
   - Right-click anywhere on the Ribbon and select **Customize the Ribbon.**
   - In the Word Options dialog box, on the right side, you'll see two columns: **Choose commands from** (left) and **Customize the Ribbon** (right).
   - Select the command you want to add from the left column and click the **Add > > button** to place it in a custom group on the Ribbon.
   - You can create new groups to organize your commands by clicking **New Group,** renaming it, and adding commands as desired.
   - **Click OK** to save your changes.

2. Removing or Renaming Ribbon Tabs:
   - In the Word Options dialog box, uncheck tabs you don't frequently use under **Customize the Ribbon.**

- To rename a tab, select it, click **Rename,** type the new name, and press **OK**.

Customizing the Quick Access Toolbar (QAT)

1. Adding Commands to the QAT:
- To add commands to the Quick Access Toolbar, right-click on any command within the Ribbon or use the dropdown arrow next to the QAT.
- Select **Add to Quick Access Toolbar** for the command to appear on the QAT at the top of the Word window.

2. Removing Commands from the QAT:
- Right-click on the command in the QAT and select **Remove from Quick Access Toolbar.**

3. Positioning the QAT:
- You can move the Quick Access Toolbar below the Ribbon by right-clicking on it and selecting **Show Below the Ribbon.**

Tips for Efficient Customization

1. Organize by Tasks: Group commands on the Ribbon and QAT by the tasks you perform most frequently, such as formatting, reviewing, or inserting objects.

2. Prioritize Frequently Used Commands: Place the most commonly used commands at the beginning of the QAT for quick access.

3. Utilize Keyboard Shortcuts: Assign shortcuts to commands on the QAT for even faster execution.

4. Exporting and Importing Customizations: Save your customizations by exporting them (Word Options > Customize Ribbon > Import/Export) and import them on another computer or after reinstalling Word.

Customizing the Ribbon and Quick Access Toolbar in Microsoft Word allows you to tailor the interface to match your workflow, making common tasks more accessible and enhancing your overall productivity. Regularly review and update these customizations based on your evolving needs to optimize your experience with Word.

Using Add-Ins

Add-ins in Microsoft Word are powerful tools that extend its functionality beyond the built-in features. They can automate tasks, provide advanced formatting options, integrate with other applications, and more.

How you can use add-ins in Microsoft Word to enhance your productivity:

Finding and Installing Add-Ins

1. Accessing Add-Ins:
   - Go to the **Insert** tab in Microsoft Word.
   - Click on **Get Add-ins** in the Add-ins group.

2. Office Add-ins Store:
   - This opens the Office Add-ins Store, where you can browse and search for add-ins categorized by function, such as productivity, education, or design.

3. Installing an Add-in:

- Click on an add-in to view details.

- Click **Add** to install it. You may need to sign in with your Microsoft account if prompted.

- The add-in will now appear under **My Add-ins** in the Insert tab.

Using Installed Add-Ins

1. Accessing Installed Add-Ins:

- After installation, access the add-in by going to the **Insert** tab > **My Add-ins.**

2. Running the Add-In:

- Select the add-in from the list to activate it. The interface and options will vary depending on the add-in functionality.

Popular Types of Add-Ins

1. Productivity Add-Ins:

- These add-ins automate common tasks like document formatting, data analysis, or email integration.

2. Collaboration Add-Ins:

- Facilitate real-time collaboration and communication within documents, such as instant messaging or shared document editing.

3. Design and Formatting Add-Ins:

- Enhance document aesthetics with advanced design tools, templates, and graphical elements.

4. Content Management Add-Ins:

- Integrate with external content management systems for seamless document sharing and version control.

Customizing Add-Ins

1. Settings and Preferences:

- Some add-ins allow customization of settings to match specific workflow needs.

- Access settings typically through the add-in interface or via the **Add-ins** section in Word Options.

2. Updating Add-Ins:
- Add-ins may receive updates from developers to improve functionality or compatibility. Update them regularly to access new features and fixes.

Security Considerations

1. Trusted Sources:
- Install add-ins only from trusted sources or the Microsoft Office Store to minimize security risks.

2. Permissions and Access:
- Review permissions required by add-ins before installation. Limit access to sensitive data if necessary.

Removing Add-Ins

1. Managing Add-Ins:

- Go to the **Insert** tab > **My Add-ins** > **See all** to manage installed add-ins.

- Remove add-ins you no longer use by clicking **Manage My Add-ins** and selecting **Remove** next to the add-in name.

Add-ins in Microsoft Word provide an array of functionalities that can significantly enhance your productivity and efficiency. By exploring and utilizing add-ins that suit your needs, you can streamline workflows, automate repetitive tasks, and customize your Word experience to better meet your professional or personal requirements.

Troubleshooting Common Issues

Troubleshooting common issues in Microsoft Word can help resolve various problems that may arise during document creation or editing.

Here are some common issues and their solutions:

1. Microsoft Word Crashes or Freezes

- Solution:

- Update Microsoft Word to the latest version via **File > Account > Update Options > Update Now.**

- Disable unnecessary add-ins that may be causing conflicts: **File > Options > Add-ins > Manage COM Add-ins > Go.**

- Check for and install Windows updates: **Settings > Update & Security > Windows Update > Check for updates.**

2. Document Formatting Issues

- Problem:

- Inconsistent formatting throughout the document.

- Unexpected layout changes.

- Solution:

- Use styles consistently: Define and apply styles for headings, paragraphs, and other elements.

- Clear formatting: Select the text, then press **Ctrl + Spacebar** to remove formatting.

3. Printing Problems

- Problem:

- Document doesn't print correctly or at all.

- Printing is slow or produces unexpected results.

- Solution:

- Check printer connections and restart the printer.

- Update printer drivers: Visit the manufacturer's website to download and install the latest drivers.

- Adjust print settings in Word: **File > Print > Printer Properties.**

4. Track Changes and Comments Issues

- Problem:

- Track Changes or comments are not visible.

- Unable to accept or reject changes.

- Solution:

- **Ensure Track Changes is enabled: Review > Track Changes > Track Changes.**

- **Show markup:** Customize how changes and comments appear in the document using **Show Markup** options in the Review tab.

5. Document Corruption or Error Messages

- Problem:

- Error messages when opening or saving documents.
- Document appears corrupted or unreadable.

- Solution:

- Use the built-in Document Recovery feature: **File > Open > Recent > Recover Unsaved Documents.**
- Copy content to a new document: Open a new document and paste content from the corrupted document.

6. Spell Check and Grammar Check Issues

- Problem:

- Spell check doesn't work or misses errors.
- Grammar suggestions are inaccurate.

- Solution:

- Check language settings: **Review > Language > Set Proofing Language.**

- Customize proofing options: **File > Options > Proofing** to adjust settings for spell check and grammar check.

7. Performance Issues

- Problem:

- Word is slow to respond or lags during use.
- Document scrolling or typing is delayed.

- Solution:

- Close unnecessary programs and background processes.

- Increase virtual memory allocation: **Control Panel > System > Advanced System Settings > Performance Settings.**

8. Compatibility and File Format Issues

- Problem:

- Unable to open documents from earlier versions of Word.

- Compatibility issues when sharing documents with others.

- Solution:

- Save documents in compatible formats: **File > Save As > Save as type** to select an appropriate format.

- Use compatibility mode: **File > Info > Compatibility Mode** to open older documents in newer versions of Word.

9. Add-In Compatibility Issues

- Problem:

- Add-ins causing Word to behave unexpectedly.

- Add-ins not functioning as expected.

- Solution:

- Disable or remove problematic add-ins: **File > Options > Add-ins > Manage COM Add-ins.**

- Check for updates to add-ins: Visit the add-in developer's website for updates or support.

General Tips for Troubleshooting

- **Restart Word:** Close and reopen Word to refresh settings and clear temporary issues.
- **Check System Requirements:** Ensure your computer meets the minimum requirements for running Microsoft Word.
- **Update Operating System:** Keep your operating system updated to ensure compatibility with Word and other software.

These troubleshooting steps, you can resolve common issues encountered while using Microsoft Word, ensuring a smoother experience and minimizing disruptions during document creation and editing. If problems persist, consider consulting Microsoft's support resources or seeking assistance from IT support professionals.

Conclusion

Mastering Microsoft Word is essential for efficient document creation, editing, and collaboration in both personal and professional settings. Throughout this guide, we've covered fundamental features, advanced techniques, and troubleshooting tips to help you navigate Word effectively.

By understanding the basics of text formatting, document layout, and utilizing tools like styles, templates, and macros, you can streamline your workflow and produce polished documents. Features such as collaboration tools, including Track Changes and real-time editing, empower teams to work seamlessly on shared documents.

Exploring advanced features such as graphics, tables, charts, and add-ins further enhances your document's visual appeal and functionality. Customizing the Ribbon, Quick Access Toolbar, and utilizing keyboard shortcuts can significantly boost productivity, saving time on routine tasks.

Moreover, troubleshooting common issues ensures that you can overcome challenges such as crashes, formatting inconsistencies, or printing problems efficiently. By staying updated with the latest software versions, maintaining good document management practices, and utilizing cloud integration for seamless sharing and storage, you can optimize your use of Microsoft Word.

Continual learning and exploration of Microsoft Word's capabilities through online resources, courses, and community forums will further enhance your skills. Whether you're a beginner or an experienced user, mastering Microsoft Word empowers you to create professional-quality documents that meet diverse needs.

Microsoft Word's versatility and robust features make it an invaluable tool for anyone needing to create, edit, and collaborate on documents effectively. Keep practicing and exploring its features to maximize your productivity and creativity in document management and communication.

Recap of Key Points

Throughout this comprehensive guide to Microsoft Word, we've covered essential topics and tips to help you become proficient in using this powerful word processing software. Here's a recap of the key points covered:

1. Introduction to Microsoft Word:
  - Microsoft Word is a versatile word processing tool used for creating, editing, formatting, and sharing documents.

2. Navigating the Interface:
  - Familiarize yourself with the Ribbon, Quick Access Toolbar, and Backstage view for efficient navigation and access to commands.

3. Basic Document Operations:

- Learn to create new documents, open and save files, and customize document properties to organize and manage your work effectively.

4. Text Formatting:

- Use text formatting tools to enhance readability and visual appeal, including font styles, sizes, colors, and alignment options.

5. Paragraph and Page Layout:

- Master paragraph formatting techniques such as indentation, line spacing, and alignment.

- Adjust page layout settings including margins, orientation, and page breaks to optimize document appearance.

6. Graphics, Tables, and Charts:

- Insert and format images, shapes, SmartArt, tables, and charts to illustrate data and enhance document presentation.

7. Advanced Features:

- Utilize advanced features such as headers and footers, page numbering, templates, and styles to standardize and streamline document creation.

8. Collaboration and Sharing:

- Collaborate effectively by using features like Track Changes, comments, and real-time editing.
- Share documents securely via cloud services like OneDrive or SharePoint.

9. Productivity Tips:

- Enhance productivity with keyboard shortcuts, customizing the Ribbon and Quick Access Toolbar, and using add-ins to extend functionality.

10. Troubleshooting and Maintenance:

- Resolve common issues like crashes, formatting problems, or printing errors using troubleshooting techniques.
- Stay updated with software updates and maintain good document management practices.

- Microsoft Word is a versatile tool for creating professional-quality documents across various industries and purposes.

- Continuous learning and exploration of Word's features will enhance your proficiency and productivity.

Applying these key points and tips, you'll be well-equipped to leverage Microsoft Word's capabilities to create, edit, and collaborate on documents efficiently, whether for personal projects, academic assignments, or professional documents.

Next Steps and Further Learning Resources

Congratulations on completing this guide to Microsoft Word! To further enhance your skills and explore more advanced features, consider the following next steps and additional learning resources:

1. Online Tutorials and Courses:

- Explore online platforms like LinkedIn Learning, Udemy, and Coursera for courses tailored to different skill levels and specific aspects of Microsoft Word.

2. Official Microsoft Documentation:

- Visit the Microsoft Office support website for comprehensive guides, tutorials, and articles on using Word effectively. The official documentation provides up-to-date information and troubleshooting tips.

3. Practice and Experiment:

- Continue practicing with Word to reinforce your knowledge of formatting, document management, and collaboration features. Experiment with different tools and settings to discover their full potential.

4. Join User Communities:

- Participate in forums, user groups, or online communities dedicated to Microsoft Office users. Engaging with others can provide valuable insights, tips, and solutions to common challenges.

5. Advanced Features Exploration:

- Dive deeper into advanced features such as macros, mail merge, advanced formatting options, and integration with other Microsoft Office applications.

6. Specialized Topics:

- Explore specialized topics such as legal document formatting, academic writing tools, desktop publishing techniques, and more based on your specific needs and interests.

7. Stay Updated:

- Keep abreast of updates and new features in Microsoft Word by subscribing to Microsoft newsletters, blogs, or following official social media channels.

8. Expand Your Toolkit:

- Explore and integrate third-party add-ins and extensions that complement your workflow and extend Word's functionality in areas like document automation, project management, or language translation.

Continued learning and exploration will help you harness the full potential of Microsoft Word, making you more efficient and effective in creating professional documents, collaborating with others, and managing your work. Embrace new challenges, seek out opportunities to expand your skills, and enjoy the benefits of mastering this essential tool for document processing and communication.

www.ingramcontent.com/pod-product-compliance
Lightning Source LLC
La Vergne TN
LVHW051333050326
832903LV00031B/3510